If I Had a Bigger Drum

If I Had a Bigger Drum

By Marjorie Lewis Lloyd

Pacific Press Publishing Association
Mountain View, California
Oshawa, Ontario

Copyright © 1981 by
Pacific Press Publishing Association
Litho in United States of America
All Rights Reserved
ISBN 0-8163-0399-1

Library of Congress Cataloging in Publication Data

Lloyd, Marjorie Lewis.
  If I had a bigger drum.

  1. Humility. I. Title.
BV4647.H8L56   241'.4   80-22491
ISBN 0-8163-0399-1

Dedication

To everyone who has ever
dreamed of leading the parade—
which is all of us!

Contents

The Drum-Major Instinct 9
Fooling the Experts 13
Love in Reverse 18
The Bluffing Game 22
Air on the Scales 28
The Pedestal People 36
Without the Silly Stilts 43
The Sinner's Declaration 51
Dismantling the Float 53
God Believes in Privacy 59
Gabriel Stands By 63
Angel Tribute 74
A Bridge Too Far 76
Unmasked 82
Total Eclipse 87
And Then the Drum 99
Of Harps and Drums 106

The Drum-Major Instinct

In the islands of the South Pacific there was a time when isolated valleys could communicate with neighboring valleys only by means of runners—and drums. Picture it. Hear it in your mind. The little man, appropriately attired or painted, beating out a skillful tattoo on his drum. Calling men to the feast, to the celebration, to worship. Warning them of the approach of enemies. Or calling them to war.

If only he had a bigger drum. More people would come to the feast. More people would come to worship. More would be warned of enemy approach. Or more would join in the battle.

But what if he longed for a bigger drum only so that more people could watch him perform—and wonder at his skill?

There are drummers less primitive, with more sophisticated instruments of communication, who with the best of motives long for a bigger drum. But there are others who use the hypnotic beat to swell the count of spectators who watch their personal parade—the parade in which *they* twirl the drumsticks for the clicking cameras.

We are all born with the drum-major instinct. What baby, from the moment he makes his premiere performance, is not the center of attention? And what child does not try to keep it that way? If the real world does not have a big enough spotlight, he will turn to the world of fantasy. "All my dreams," said one little girl, "come out the same way. I'm always somebody important."

Do we ever quite grow out of it? Why do we want to paint or preach or sing? To help people, of course. Who would dare to suggest any other motive? Yet praise never makes us unhappy—even if we don't deserve it. We like the sound of it even when we don't believe it. It doesn't bother us at all unless we hear too much of it directed to somebody else.

Madison Avenue knows all about the drum-major instinct. That's why we get letters that say, "You have been selected to receive the accompanying brochure because we have learned that you are a highly intellectual individual who is interested in world affairs, in good literature, in art and in science." Of course we'll read on. It describes us so precisely. That's the way we get hooked.

The drum-major instinct. The desire to be somebody. The urge to be important. That's why we join exclusive clubs and drop names and drive expensive cars and put stickers on our luggage. That's why we eat at the best restaurants. That's why we collect ribbons and medals and trophies—and degrees.

In a nation without a king there are thousands who try to be king anyway. They crave the pomp and pageantry that go with royalty. And so they beat their own drums and elbow themselves into high position, certain that fitness will come with landing the job.

In the days of President Taft's administration a woman who knew the President personally kept urging him to appoint her husband to the post of Secretary of Commerce. Her husband was a house painter. The President tried tactfully to suggest that the job required a big man, a man with long preparation for its demands. But she saw no problem. It would all take care of itself. If the President would only appoint him to the position, he *would be* a big man!

Doesn't a big chair make a big man? Won't buying an organ make you an accomplished organist in two or three weeks? Won't buying the right camera make you an expert cameraman with all the creativeness of a *Life* magazine photographer? All you have to do is read the instructions!

This urge to be in the spotlight, to lead the parade, can get out of hand. It can work havoc with the personality. Some timid people become unpleasantly aggressive. And some are so tormented by being little that they boast themselves taller and taller until we pity them. Some try to get ahead by pushing other people back.

Many a crime is committed by frustrated individuals who find no other way to get attention. With a gun in their hand they are fearless. Without it, they are frightened little men.

In Hitler and Mussolini the drum-major instinct went berserk. It is said that Mussolini, asked what his ambition was, replied, "I am obsessed by one wild desire. It consumes my whole being. I want to make a mark on my era with my will. A mark like this." And then with his fingernails he scratched the back of a chair from end to end. "Like the claw of a lion!"

And Hitler? He left a trail of blood and tears across Europe!

The drum-major instinct. Better known as pride.

Who was it who first allowed pride to grow in his heart? Grow to such an extent that he had to be cast out of heaven. He came to our planet where he has been practicing his trade for some 6000 years!

Look around you if you will. See the newest scars on this planet of ours. The most recent hurricane. The most devastating fire. The earthquake that is freshest in your mind. Multiply it all a thousand times. And multiply again. Pride did it.

Listen to the heartcry of a hurting world. A world of separations and good-byes. A world trying to understand the crashing planes, the loss of innocent children, the shattering of dreams. Take the hurts of your own heart. Multiply them by all that memory holds. And then by a planet. Pride did it.

Sense if you can the enormity of the mess we're in. Pride did it. That's how deadly it is. Pride in the heart of one angel. Pride is back of the whole show!

There isn't a soul who hasn't been touched by the contamination of pride. The fallen angel has instilled it into every heart, where it can be removed only by the miracle of divine surgery.

We are proud of how we look, proud of our accomplishments, proud of our degrees. Proud of how young we are or how old we are or how many years we have worked. Proud that we aren't retired. Proud that we aren't stupid. Proud of how many miles we can jog. Proud of the important people we know. Proud of where we've been or where we are or where we are going. Some people are even proud of how bad they once were!

Have I missed anything? A few thousand things!

Every one of us would like to have a bigger drum. And we are sure our motives are right. We want it only so we can do more good. We have good news for the world. And we could tell it quicker and farther if we had a bigger drum!

But there is such a subtle line between wanting power for the sake of other people and wanting it for ourselves. It's a line so difficult to see!

I've never read a book about pride. Have you? But since pride got us into all this trouble, I thought there ought to be one.

So in these pages I'm going to throw out some missiles—not at proud people, but at pride itself. You can stay by and watch the fun if you like—and be glad the missiles aren't meant for you.

On the other hand, you just may discover that you are afflicted like the rest of us. If you do, I dare you to admit it and point your finger in reverse and do something about it!

By the way, along with the missiles there will be a lot of hope!

The way I see it is this. If these pages should lead even a few to defect from the camp of the proud and seek asylum among the humble, then the book won't have to be a best seller to be a roaring success!

Fooling the Experts

The strange, bizarre story begain in the spring of 1967, when Elmyr de Hory, sick, and hounded by debts, shared his life story with a neighbor on the island of Ibiza. The result was that the neighbor, Clifford Irving, wrote a book about de Hory. It was titled simply *Fake*.

Elmyr de Hory was an artist, a genius—but not a creative genius. Rather, he was a genius at copying, at faking. To show Clifford Irving what he could do, he turned out three drawings one morning before lunch—two Matisse and a Modigliani. Irving took them to the Museum of Modern Art, told the curators he had inherited them from an aunt, and asked them to see if the drawings were genuine. After studying them for two hours the curators said they were absolutely genuine. They seemed horrified, Irving said, that he wanted to sell the drawings.

Elmyr de Hory is known as the master art forger of our time. During twenty years and throughout five continents he sold about a thousand works of art and took in millions of dollars. When his game finally ended, a Paris newspaper estimated that if his fakes were to be sold at 1968 market prices, they would probably bring as much as 60 million dollars.

Clifford Irving's book about de Hory was a success. He sent a copy of it to Howard Hughes, he said, and Hughes was so impressed that he asked him to do his autobiography. The wheels of the great hoax had already begun to turn in his mind. And it ought not to be too great a risk. If Howard Hughes would rather lose a court case than make a public appearance, certainly he wouldn't emerge from seclusion to challenge an autobiography.

There followed an almost unbelievable saga of forged signatures, forged letters, huge checks, and a fake manuscript that left a lot of people red-faced. It fooled *Life* magazine. It fooled McGraw-Hill. It fooled the handwriting people. Even after the hoax came apart, as hoaxes eventually do, it appeared that the story of it, the details of how it had been carried out, might bring its perpetrator as much as a million dollars.

Said Clifford Irving: "All the world loves to see the experts and the establishment made a fool of. And everyone likes to feel that those who set themselves up as experts are really just as gullible as anybody else."

I'm not so sure that the world approves a hoax. Rather, I think what we are seeing may be simply a growing feeling that there is phoniness at the top, that the experts sometimes do some faking of their own.

And Clifford Irving's was not the first literary fake to receive public admiration. A publisher once asked the writer Herbert Mayes to do a biography of Horatio Alger, the popular novelist who died in 1899. Mayes looked into the subject and found it wasn't worth writing about. Alger, he said, "was a dope, a dull idiot who wrote dreadful books." But the publisher suggested he do the biography anyway. So Mayes invented for Alger a fantastically exciting life, and the book was published in 1928. It was all fiction. He had made it all up. Yet Mayes never spent any time in jail. Instead, he went on to become editor of such publications as *McCall's* and *Good Housekeeping*.

In the '60s Mayes publicly confessed the hoax to the Horatio Alger Society. But the society, instead of being outraged, in 1975 made him an honorary member!

Then there was D. B. Cooper, the skyjacker who bailed out the back door of a Northwest Orient 727 and vanished—with $200,000 strapped to his chest. The American public seemed to regard him as more of a hero than an outlaw. A sociology professor at the University of Washington commented that the hijacker had won public admiration because he pulled off "an awesome feat in the battle of man against the machine—one individual overcoming, for the time being anyway, technology, the corporation, the establishment, the system."

A Portland company, riding the wave of publicity, marketed T-shirts glamorizing the piracy. One shirt carried the slogan, "Skyjacking, the Only Way to Fly."

And then there was the amazing episode at a Mexican jail. A helicopter landed boldly in the courtyard of the prison, took aboard several inmates, and took off again without being challenged. Watching officers simply saluted, thinking them VIPs.

Again, there seems to be something in the makeup of today's society that likes to see the experts fooled. And who of us has not tried to do a little fooling ourselves?

Said one writer, "Modern society trains us to be subtle and sophisticated, indirect and devious, clever. We live by exaggeration and affectation. We become experts at impression, masters at pretense. We can tell the truth while living the lie. And what dupes we delight to be! Just glance discerningly at the pages of advertising in some popular periodical!

"We lie by the way we walk, the way we dress, the way we laugh. We lie by the inflection of our voices. Both our speech and our silence are calculated to deceive. We express emotions we do not feel, and our acted-out virtues are often our egotistical fascination with the possibility of rising momentarily to another's expectations, to dominate another's opinion by our own deceit. How seldom we seem to realize that a lie is always a liability. We prefer the world of make-believe. We take fiendish delight in playing a trick on real life as often as we can!"

Madison Avenue has made us so familiar with exaggeration and pretense that we hardly notice it. For instance, did it ever trouble you at all that this Eastern Air Lines commerical is all make-believe? "Come. We will be your wings. We will set you free. Free beyond the heights of man. Free to chase the sun. Hug a cloud. . . ."

People like to pretend. A clever hoax disturbs them only if they themselves are victims. They flock to the movies, or crowd around their television sets, to watch people pretend.

And they like to pretend themselves. They pretend they are not home when they are. They pretend they are richer than they are, for the neighbors—and poorer than they are, for the IRS. Yet everybody knows it is wrong to pretend. Even as far as we are from Eden and the image of God, we still sense that there is something not right about pretending.

A Beverly Hills psychiatrist, with many Hollywood actors and actresses among his patients, was asked what is tormenting the actors. "Guilt," said Dr. Greenson. "One, he feels guilty because showing your body is not accepted in our society. Two, he feels guilty because it's wrong to be a pretender. Three, there's guilt for what he is unconsciously doing to the audience. . . . He has enormous reasons for guilt."

Dr. Greenson believes that an audience feels both envy and contempt for actors. "Our contempt," he says, "is due to the fact that the actor devotes his life to pretending. He pretends to be so-and-so, and he's not really so-and-so. That's 'lying.' That's hypocrisy."

Wrong to pretend. Yet for the proud man the big temptation is to be accepted and applauded for what he is not. His name may never be picked up by the press. But in his own little world he is king. He has his court, his admirers, and his kingdom, small or large. It may involve half a dozen people—or a million. But they stand by him loyally until he is exposed as a fraud, a pretender, a usurper of the throne. And sometimes they keep on believing even then.

This temptation to be something he is not, is not peculiar to the big-time operator. A man may be fooling only his own family. And he may be fooling only himself. But the urge to pretend is strong. And Satan, the master pretender, will not let him go easily. His chains can be broken only by the Lord Jesus Christ.

Said Jesus, "So if the Son sets you free, you will be free indeed." John 8:36, N.I.V.

But Jesus sets no man free who does not want to be free.

Thousands bluff their way through life, never quite willing to acknowledge their chains. Like the Pharisees of Christ's day, they protest, "We are Abraham's descendants and have never been slaves of anyone. How can you say that we shall be set free?" John 8:33, N.I.V.

And so the Saviour turns, with tears, and waits. He waits for captive men and women to hear the clank of their own chains and call out, "Lord, save me!"

But the tragedy of sin is that millions never will. They will die slaves—when they could have been free!

Love in Reverse

We hear a strange noise in the night. It could be a thief. We pick up the telephone and call for help. A series of crimes has brought terror to our neighborhood. We ask the police for extra protection. Fire breaks out—and we salvage what we can. The fury of the hurricane or the ruthlessness of the earthquake tears down the house of our dreams. And we call the insurance adjuster.

But all these are nothing when placed beside the real danger. No thief can steal the things that matter most. No fire can burn, no wind can blow away the fabric of your faith. Pride is the ruthless fiend you need to fear. It is pride that strangles love and blinds men to their need and fixes them in front of the mirror where they can see nothing but self. It is pride that will jam hell with its victims!

Jesus said, "Do not be afraid of those who kill the body but cannot kill the soul. Rather, be afraid of the one who can destroy both soul and body in hell." Matthew 10:28, N.I.V.

Who is it who will destroy soul and body in hell? Is it really God? Or is it Satan—or self—or pride?

Abraham Lincoln, asked about the possibility of his being elected President, said this: "I have no fear for Breckinridge, he is a Southerner, the North will not support him. I'm not worrying about Douglas, the South is against him. My greatest worry is that man named Lincoln. If I am defeated, it will be by that man."

Well said?

Pride is love in reverse. It is love turned the wrong way, turned in instead of out. And when love operates in reverse, it comes out as squeaky and as senseless as a tape being rewound.

But pride is more than ludicrous. It is dangerous. It is the deadliest of poisons. It lies at the foundation of all sin.

Pride is self-love. It is self-idolatry. It is the self-made man worshiping his own creator.

Yet self-love is promoted in our society with all the zeal of a Madison Avenue agency. Love yourself, we are told. Discover yourself. Find the real you. Discover the power within. Accept yourself. Believe in yourself. Forgive yourself. Be happy with yourself. Be happy that God made you just as you are. Feel good about yourself. Join the I'm-OK crowd. All the negative emotions—like anger and fear and grief—stem from the lack of self-love. Only if you love yourself can you love anyone else. God left it to you to create yourself and your world.

That's the line that we hear like a broken record. And millions accept it. They look into the mirror and decide they are looking at the answer to the world's dilemma. God must be lucky to have them around. They go looking for a job. And they tell each other, "You have so much to offer. Don't settle for anything but the best." And when the prospective employers don't see what they see, they come home and lick their wounds and decide that the world just isn't ready for a person with their unique talents.

Self-love is said to be the way to success. But is it? Yes—success is utterly deceiving ourselves, making a fool of ourselves.

When a man begins to worship himself, when he decides that he himself is a god or a part of God, it means simply that he is a victim of the cleverest and most subtle con game ever played. All this ballyhoo about loving yourself is the philosophy of the fallen angel. For that's where it started. And that's what made him a devil.

Pride is a sickness—a sickness more nearly incurable than any other.

How do we save ourselves from the sickness of pride? We

don't and we can't. And that's why the popular remedies, the most promoted remedies for the problems of our day, don't work. They turn us inward for the answers. And the more we take of the supposed cure, the sicker we are!

The cure doesn't work, because its active ingredient is the venom of the serpent. Yet the saddest thing of all is that Jesus is widely believed to have prescribed it. Didn't he say, "Love your neighbor as yourself"?

Yes. *As* yourself. But He didn't say, "Love yourself." He didn't even say, "Love your neighbor *and* yourself." He knew that human nature has no deficiency of self-love. Most of us love ourselves far too much. His own disciples were so afflicted with self-love, with wanting to be the greatest, that the early church was in danger of being wrecked before it got started. Jesus was simply telling us to love our neighbor the way we are inclined to love ourselves. There's quite a difference!

Open your Bible. The teaching of Jesus is there for all to read. He told the people not to take the highest seats. He told them that pride defiles a man. The way to be great, He said, is to be a servant. He called the proud Pharisees actors and said everything they did was done for show. And He said, "Every man who promotes himself will be humbled, and every man who learns to be humble will find promotion." Matthew 23:12, Phillips.

We will never find the love-yourself philosophy in the teaching of Jesus. It was the serpent who introduced it to this world. And he lost no time in doing it. It was in the Garden of Eden that he tried out his two-pronged propaganda on Eve. And it worked so well he has been using it ever since.

"Ye shall not surely die." And "ye shall be as gods." There it is. The serpent has the world pretty well convinced that death never really happens. And he's doing very well with his second falsehood, "Ye shall be as gods."

Wouldn't it be a tragedy if we who have so carefully avoided the first trap, who have worked so diligently to expose the first falsehood—wouldn't it be a tragedy if we, of all people, should be caught up in the second?

Self-improvement is not the answer. No amount of fixing

over, painting over, or diligent repairing will ever give us characters fit for heaven. We need a miracle from outside ourselves. We need a miracle of creative power. And that we do not have. To try to make ourselves great is only to make ourselves a laughingstock. And to try to make ourselves important is to make ourselves insigificant.

It's even more serious than that. A self-centered existence is the principle of Satan's rebellion. Then to live a self-centered life is to live a Satan-centered life. Can it be otherwise?

The fallen angel's one object is to steal away from God the worship that is due Him. Every temptation that comes to us has in it the invitation to go it alone, to depend on self, to make self the object of worship.

And you can count on it. The wily tempter will trip you up if he can. Every step you take in the right direction, he will be right there with his flattering persuasion. He'll whisper in your ear, "That was a right good job you did. You're wonderful. Don't you know you're really great?"

And listen. The moment you start agreeing with him, you've had it!

The Bluffing Game

A videotape control room is not exactly a place to relax. There is always a certain amount of tension. The director, especially, aware that a large share of responsibility for the finished product rests with him, may be a little abrupt. At least this was the atmosphere I had come to expect.

Then one day it all changed. It was a new season, with a new director. He had come highly recommended. All should go well. I remember the first day. He sat down and put on his earphones—smiling, confident, relaxed—and the program was under way. How different. Everything was calm, quiet, smooth. Evidently a control room didn't have to be a place of tension—if you had a director who knew his business. Here was competence. And I was glad.

For several days it went the same way—smooth. The programs seemed to be coming out all right. Only one little thing puzzled me. Several times I suggested to the director that we really should have some dissolves in certain places—not all cuts. But each time he told me, "Your program is just not the type for dissolves. They really don't fit your program."

He was such a friendly fellow and seemed so competent that it hardly seemed right to argue the point—even if we were the ones who were paying for the program.

Then one day a technician called me out of the control room. He wanted to speak to me privately. There was something I should know. I learned then that what had seemed like competence had been an ultra-smooth job of bluffing. The director's seven years of experience had been all office experience. He knew nothing about videotape. And all he knew about directing was where to sit, how to put on his earphones, and how to open the line between himself and the technicians. He had been doing little more than listening—while long-suffering technicians who felt sorry for him did his job!

How could it have happened? I had talked personally to his superior, under whom he had worked those years. Evidently the executive just couldn't bring himself to tell me the truth about the man's lack of know-how in the field of videotape. How can you expose such a nice fellow?

The dissovles? The truth would have come out shortly anyway. A special film segment in which dissolves were essential had to be prepared. And somebody had to come and sit in his chair and take over. He simply didn't have the faintest idea how to do a dissolve. That was why they didn't fit our program.

The bluffing game is never at a loss for players. Its persistent participants—both fellows and non-fellows—will put on a show for you any day. No appointment necessary.

Mr. Bluff, for instance, wanted a chance to do some specialty work for Company A, but he lacked the experience. So he went to Company B, Company C, and Company D and managed to give them the idea that he was already doing work for Company A. Impressed, since they knew the high demands of Company A, they all gave him small contracts. Then Mr. Bluff went back to Company A and argued that he certainly ought to be qualified for a contract because he was doing work for Companies B, C, and D.

Postscript. The ruse didn't work.

You know the bluffers as well as I. The men who get jobs because of experience they never had—and promotions because of the work their secretaries do. The highly paid secretaries who can't even write a letter. People who graciously accept compliments, paychecks, and promotions for work they never did.

Often it's the fellow with the biggest blow who gets the

biggest job and the highest pay. And yet don't feel too sorry for his employer. For some employers are more interested in blow than efficiency.

Some bluffing is just a harmless part of growing up. Harley Rice, a friend of mine who is no longer with us, told a delightful little story on himself. When he was a very young man, his father sent him a briefcase for Christmas. It was his very first briefcase, and he was very proud of it. He was a bookkeeper at Paradise Valley Sanitarium at the time, and a meeting was called in Los Angeles. It was the first business meeting of any consequence he had been asked to attend. He went to Glendale on the train—he and his new briefcase. He didn't have a thing to put in it; so he stuffed it with paper.

He was to stay at the Glendale Sanitarium. E. G. Fulton, the manager met him in the lobby and took him to his room, which was in the basement. The manager insisted on carrying Harley's briefcase for him—that new briefcase full of stuffing. But of course he didn't know. And the fact that somebody important had carried Harley's briefcase took all the curse off sleeping in the basement. Said Harley, telling of the experience, "If we can understand in deep charity how vain we all are, then we will never knowingly humiliate or belittle another." And he continued, "For this same reason, knowing our vanity, kind people will always give others a face-saving way out from any embarrassing position in which they may find themselves."

Yes, we do some strange things because of vanity. We are all afflicted. I wish we were all as understanding, and as kind, as Harley Rice. Face-saving is so very important—for ourselves. But we're perfectly willing to let the other fellow get the humiliating spotlight!

And if only our problem were limited to a little briefcase stuffing. But it is nothing so trivial. We stuff our minds with our own self-importance—and then can't understand why our obvious goodness doesn't have the impact on others that we imagine it should. Humble? Of course. We wear humility beautifully—don't you think?

When the prophet Isaiah was given a vision of God's glory, he had no inclination to boast of his own goodness. Rather, he responded, "Woe is me! for I am undone; because I am a man of unclean lips . . . : for mine eyes have seen the King, the Lord of hosts." Isaiah 6:5.

Commenting on Isaiah's words, Ellen White says, "This is not that voluntary humility and servile self-reproach that so many seem to consider it a virtue to display. This vague mockery of humility is prompted by hearts full of pride and self-esteem. There are many who demerit themselves in words, who would be disappointed if this course did not call forth expressions of praise and appreciation from others."—*S.D.A. Bible Commentary*, vol. 4, p. 1140.

Jesus despised hypocrisy—bluffing—even in a fig tree. Telling a lie with its leaves. Pretending to bear fruit. To Jesus it was trickery.

Was it an accident that the cursing of the fig tree was followed by the cleansing of the temple? Was not the fruitless tree an appropriate symbol of what was wrong in the temple, in Jerusalem, in the nation that Jesus called His own? The sin of Jerusalem, of Israel, was not so much in its fruitlessness as in its colossal pretense—in pretending to long for the coming of the Messiah, while they rejected the Messiah who had come. The sin of the temple was in making the house of prayer a place for slick business, for get-rich-quick schemes, for under-the-counter cheating, for exploiting the poor and the innocent. The house of sacrifice had become a carnival of extortion. And they called it salvation!

If Jesus was unhappy with the commercializing of the temple, He was also unhappy with its prayers. Remember the Pharisee and the publican?

The villain, of course is the Pharisee who publicly thanks God that he is not like the tax collector standing over there. But the Pharisee has left a big family. A Sunday School teacher told her class about the Pharisee and the publican. And then she said, "Now, children, let us thank God that we are not like that Pharisee."

And wait! What were you thinking just then? Were you thanking God that you were not like that teacher? On and on it goes. Who of us can claim to be free from pride?

David Redding, one of my favorite authors, said it so well:

"The better the man, the better he can see what is wrong with him. The first sign of the saint is this highly developed sense of sin. The Pharisee is proud he is not like other men. The saint hangs his head that he is not like Christ!"

If only we were like Christ. If only we were so in love with Him that we could think of nothing else. If only we knew Him as it is our privilege to know Him. Then we would have something to tell the world!

Dare I ask it? Is it possible that it is in our witnessing for Christ that we are most guilty of playing the bluffing game?

G. W. Target in his book *The Window and Other Essays* tells the story of a man in a hospital, whose bed was near a window. He was the only patient in the ward who could see out the window. So day after day he described for the patient next to him the beautiful grounds, the birds and the flowers, the lake in the distance, the children playing.

But one day the man died, and the patient next to him was moved into his bed. Now he could see for himself. With great effort he managed to prop himself up until he could see out. Imagine his surprise to see that there was nothing there—only a blank wall. His fellow-patient had been describing that which he himself did not see. The bluffing game again!

Have you ever read these words? "Servants of God, with their faces lighted up and shining with holy consecration, will hasten from place to place to proclaim the message from heaven. By thousands of voices, all over the earth, the warning will be given. Miracles will be wrought, the sick will be healed, and signs and wonders will follow the believers. . . .

"The message will be carried not so much by argument as by the deep conviction of the Spirit of God. . . . Now the rays of light penetrate everywhere, the truth is seen in its clearness, and the honest children of God sever the bands which have held them. Family connections, church relations, are powerless to stay them now. Truth is more precious than all besides. Notwithstanding the agencies combined against the truth, a large number take their stand upon the Lord's side."—*The Great Controversy*, p. 612.

This, says the inspired pen, is what will happen. Why isn't it happening now? Because it isn't time yet? Or because our faces aren't shining yet? Is it because we are only bluffing about our relationship with Jesus? Are we trying to lead others into an experience of which we know nothing? Is that why people aren't listening?

If only we were a people of prayer! If only we would spend so much time with Jesus that our faces would begin to shine with the reflected glory of His countenance! Then people would listen. And Jesus could return!

Air on the Scales

Muhammad Ali, hosting a television special, began with these words: "When you're host of a show—like I am tonight—it isn't good to be braggin' about yourself. So tonight I'm not goin' to do it. Tonight I'm goin' to be humble. I'm goin' to do it. Because there's nothin'—just *nothin'*—that I can't do!"

We smile at Muhammad Ali. We can smile because he knows as well as we how ridiculous his words are. But what of those who go around saying "I am the greatest"—and don't know what a laughable but sorry picture they make?

In Jesus' day the problem was "*Who* is the greatest?" Today it is simply "*I* am the greatest." It's "How do I look, everybody?" We are often more concerned about how we *look* doing our job than how we are *doing* our job. Buy a boat. And then how much you know about navigation doesn't matter. But be sure you have an admiral's cap!

Image is the word today. Not how good we *are*, but how good we *look*. What will people think? What will the press say? What will this do to my vote? The role of the makeup man becomes more and more important.

But can you imagine Einstein asking his friends how long a great scientist ought to grow his hair? Can you imagine Noah climbing to a high platform beside the ark and beginning his appeal, "Now, people, I feel that I am well qualified to speak on this subject because I am, after all, the world's most eminent shipbuilder"?

It is said that H. A. Rowland was once called upon to testify as a science expert in some kind of court case. An attorney, exploring the extent of his competence, asked him who was the foremost American physicist. Rowland answered unhesitatingly, "I am." Later a friend gently reproached him for being so immodest, and Rowland replied, "Well, you have to remember I was under oath."

Everybody wants to be first. Nobody wants to be second. Someone has suggested that if all the automobiles in the United States were lined up bumper to bumper, 250,000 miles of them, 93 percent of their drivers would immediately pull out to pass. The length of the line may be out of date, but is the percentage far off?

This desire to be first, this hunger for self-importance, finds such shabby and pathetic ways of reaching for the top. Shoving others out of the way, pushing themselves ahead. Seeking the appearance of importance without possessing the reality. Criticizing others in a backhanded bid for self-promotion. Trying to climb by pulling the other fellow down. Belittling whatever one feels inferior to. The unconscious scramble for chief seats. The ill-disguised attempt to exalt self by devaluating others. The perpetual complimenting of self with or without visible reason for such satisfaction. The ruthlessness of pride. It all becomes an obsession, a deep sickness tht is obvious to all but the patient.

Psychiatrists say that one of the ruling motives in mental illness is the obsessive desire to be free from the torment of inferiority. And criminologists have learned to look for this obsession in the murderer, the terrorist, the juvenile delinquent. It is the pathological desire of the little man to be big.

We tire so soon of the trumpets of the proud, the beating of their drums. The mask is so thin and the motive so obvious. Yet the proud man seldom realizes how he looks to others.

Dr. Harry Emerson Fosdick, in his autobiography, tells how John D. Rockefeller, Jr., arrived at church on a Sunday morning a little later than usual. The service had already begun. He said to the usher, "I won't go to my regular pew this morning. I may disturb the service. I'll find a seat in the balcony." At that moment a pompous and aggressive stranger, not recognizing Mr. Rockefeller, stepped up and said to the usher, "Show me. I'll take a seat downstairs. I'm not the balcony type."

Pride is ugly. It is pitiful. It is not a pretty picture. Why stop to look at it? Why dwell on its ugliness? Because pride is not only ugly, it is lethal. We need to know the symptoms—so that we can recognize them in ourselves. Because pride can kill us—forever!

Divine surgery is our only hope. But who of us would submit to surgery without first being convinced of the seriousness of our affliction? That's why we have to look at pride. Ugly. Unlovely. Sometimes amusing. But always pitiful. Because pride kills!

Pride professes deep concern for people. It has always been that way. You remember that Lucifer professed a deep concern for the angels. But the proud man's interest in people often involves only what people can do for him, how they can be used to further his own career.

Listen to the talk-show hosts on radio if you want some examples. They will gladly tell you how much they care. But their caring seems to be all one-way. Frequently they are abrupt and rude and cut people off mercilessly. They are interested in their own image. They want to be known for a fast-moving show. And some of them are so anxious to keep it fast that their greetings and responses to callers are reduced to little more than grunts. They seem to be saying, "Hurry up and say something so I can cut you off."

In contrast, I have sometimes listened late at night to one who is refreshingly different. He doesn't talk about much that is very profound, but it is obvious that he loves people. And even when he has to ease a crackpot off the air, he does it so kindly and so gently that the most sensitive soul could not take offense. But he is an exception.

Just the other day I heard statistics presented that purported to show that a man's success is related to his height, that tall men—and tall women—are more successful. Adam was tall—and Eve. But would we really say that Eve was successful?

Isaac Watts, the great hymn writer, was small in stature. He was once riding in a parade in the city of London. A woman who watched from an open window was so astonished not to see a tall man that she said aloud, "What! You Isaac Watts?" And he heard her. He stopped the carriage, stood to his feet, spread his short arms in a gesture of wideness, and said in rhyme,

> Could I in fancy reach the pole
> Or grasp creation in my span,
> I'd still be measured by my soul;
> The mind's the measure of the man.

The prophet Samuel said to Saul, "Time was when you thought little of yourself, but now you are head of the tribes of Israel, and the Lord has anointed you king over Israel." 1 Samuel 15:17, N.E.B.

It was in that same conversation that Samuel said, "The Lord has rejected you as king over Israel." Verse 26.

It was when Saul was little in his own eyes that he was made king. He was a proud man when he was rejected.

Little in our own eyes. But humanity doesn't like to be little. Pride wants to be big—in its own eyes if not in the eyes of others.

Do you know the first thing that pride does when it takes a new job? A proud man will already have settled on the matter of a salary appropriate for his unique talents. But once on the job he will be concerned with how his name will appear on the door, on his letterheads, on his cards, in the company advertising. He will be concerned with how the credits will read along before he has done any work to be credited for. He will want to be sure that his title at least doubles his ability.

Call this a parable if you like: A proud man took over a small printshop in the days when type was still set by hand. He wanted to be sure that every piece of work reflected only his own ability, not that of his predecessor. So he dumped all the fonts of type in one big heap. Sometimes he had to search for hours to find a letter he wanted. And if he had a pressing deadline, he was even known to call his predecessor to find what he couldn't find. Just a parable. But, with certain variations, it happened.

Pride leads a man to do strange things. And it gives him strange and unreasonable prejudices.

An associate and I were looking over some artwork that had been prepared by a team of artists. It was excellent work, but I was surprised to hear this candid comment: "There is just one thing I can't reconcile. They're women." He just couldn't accept the fact that such fine work had been done by women artists.

I was only slightly acquainted with this man; so I had been unaware of his personal prejudices. I said, "Do you have a thing about women?" He said, "All men do."

Unimportant, you say? Trivial? Yes. But there are men among us, proud men, who simply can't reconcile themselves to the fact that in the last century God selected a woman to be His special messenger. And when a man begins to question God's actions, God's decisions, God's choices, is that trivial? Is that a little thing? Or is it an indication of how severe a sickness pride can be?

There are men holding jobs today whose only qualification for their work is that they wear a necktie. And there are proud men among us who, if reincarnation were for real, certainly must have spent their past life in studying how not to be born a woman. Is this an unimportant fact of life? Have I wandered onto forbidden ground? Or is it a symptom of pride that ought to be dealt with on bended knee?

"The trouble with Ralph Nader," said on critic, "is that he thinks he's God." It seems to me a cruel assessment in Ralph Nader's case. But all of us have known those whom the criticism fits. We have all been amused and saddened by the sight of men on paper thrones with kindergarten crowns. The one-man parades and the phony ticker tape. The seventy-six trombones. The silver trophies men give to themselves. The self-glory sessions. The loud horns. The thundering exhaust. The juvenile exhibitions of power. The games in which most of the time one man is "it." The friendly reminder, carefully casual, "You can call me 'doctor' now if you like."

George Eliot said of a proud man, "He was like a cock who thought the sun had risen to hear him crow."

Why is it that success, prosperity, two or three extra letters behind his name—why is it that these seldom make a man better, they just make him proud? And why is it that the finest people are the least concerned about proving that they are the finest.

A woman who had just been appointed chief justice of a state supreme court sent an aide out to find an apartment for her. The aide found one that was satisfactory, but the landlady refused to rent to the justice without recommendations. When the justice learned this, she laughed and said, "They let anybody on the court these days." And then, seriously, she promised to try not to mistake herself for her title.

Good advice for all of us?

But enough of this. What does God think of all our self-praise, our bombastic boasting? I found out several years ago when I came across these words of David, as paraphrased in Kenneth Taylor's *The Living Bible:* "The greatest of men, or the lowest—both alike are nothing in his sight. They weigh less than air on scales." Psalm 62:9.

Less than air on scales! Yes, I know that air does have weight. But not enough to show up on your scales or mine. Or God's.

Men may throw their weight around and sweep everything and everyone ahead of them like a tornado. But when God one day asks these human tornadoes to step on the scales, they will not weigh very much. Even then, unfortunately, some will not see the truth. They think they stand too tall.

Evidently the apostle Paul agreed with David; for he said, "If anyone thinks he is something when he is nothing, he deceives himself." Galatians 6:3, N.I.V.

And he asked the penetrating question that we so persistently forget: "For who makes you different from anyone else? What do you have that you did not receive? And if you did receive it, why do you boast as though you did not?" 1 Corinthians 4:7, N.I.V.

And Jesus said, "Be careful not to do your 'acts of righteousness' before men, to be seen by them. If you do, you will have no reward from your Father in heaven. So when you give to the needy, do not announce it with trumpets, as the hypocrites do in the synagogues and on the streets, to be honored by men. I tell you the truth, they have received their reward in full." Matthew 6:1, 2, N.I.V.

"They have received their reward in full." Sad, sad words!

It was an inspired pen that wrote "Every man who praises himself, brushes the luster from his best efforts."—*Testimonies,* vol. 4, p. 607.

And from the same pen we read, "In place of the righteousness and perfection of the infinite God, the true object of adoration; in place of the perfect righteousness of His law, the true standard of human attainment, Satan has substituted the sinful, erring nature of man himself as the only object of adoration, the only rule of judgment, or standard of character. This is progress, not upward, but downward. . . .

". . . Man will never rise higher than his standard of purity or goodness or truth. If self is his loftiest ideal, he will never attain to anything more exalted. Rather, he will constantly sink lower and lower."—*The Great Controversy,* p. 555.

Ought we not to forget our mad scramble for bigger drums until we are ready to beat them for a better cause than self? Ought we not to forget the rationalizing and defending and explaining away of our sins, trying to make them look white to others—when we need so desperately to be on our knees confessing them, acknowledging how black they are?

What does it matter how many years we serve, how many books we write, how many sermons we preach, how many tears we shed—if those tears and those years are polluted by pride? All these, if contaminated by self-worship, will not weigh an ounce on the scales of heaven. Pride makes everything we do unacceptable to God and ineffective in our witness to men.

In the final day God will look only at the condition of our hearts. He will ask, "Is pride gone?" He will look to see if there is a germ of it left that would reinfect heaven. For make no mistake. God will not take that risk. He will not overlook in us the same pride that cost Lucifer his high position!

He will not overlook it. But He will gladly take it away—if we are willing.

The man I want to hear, the man that will get me on the

front seat, the man whose words will hold me spellbound, is the man whose face is shining because he has been with Jesus. It's the man who has been to his knees and stayed there until he is a new creation. It's the man who has been to the cross and found out how little he is and how big God is. It's the man who has been to the Book and discovered his true self—discovered that his heart is desperately wicked, that all have sinned, that there is none righteous but his Lord, that his whole head is sick, that his own best efforts are like polluted garments, that he is helpless and lost without the miracle that only God can accomplish. It's the man who can say "I was wrong" and mean it—and not cancel out his confession with qualifications that neutralize all his tears. He, to me—and I believe to God—is a truly great man!

Pride. It's an ugly thing, a negative thing. It is not a pretty picture. But sometimes revealing must come before healing. And one of the most positive, helpful, healing, hopeful things we can do is to walk up close to Jesus—close enough to see the scars in His hands, close enough to see how little we are, how unclean we are, how desperately lost we are unless we will let Him cut away our pride. It's the most important discovery we could ever make. And the Lord Jesus has waited a long time for us to make it!

The Pedestal People

A skillful architect was once commissioned to build a watchtower for the pharaoh of Egypt. His name was Cnidius. While the building was in process, he had his own name engraved in large letters on a stone in the wall. Then he covered his name with mortar and engraved the pharaoh's name in golden characters on the outside. All was done, of course, for the glory and honor of the pharaoh. So he pretended. But the architect well knew that time and weather would remove the outer plastering. It would be his own name and memory that would remain for future generations.

Could it be that there are some today who are promoting self under the thin veneer of promoting Christ? Is it possible that some whose lives have been set apart for the services of Christ are actually hoping that the name of Jesus will wear away just enough to let their own name appear? There is such a subtle line between preaching Christ and preaching self. And it's a line, a vital distinction, that a man on a pedestal is frequently unable to discern.

No one on earth is in more danger than the minister who is popular with the people—and popular with himself. Satan will tell him every chance he gets that he is surely God's great gift to humanity. And the minute a man begins to believe it, both he and his pedestal are perilously near the precipice. The tragedy is that such a man stands too tall to see the devil cutting away the props beneath him. And so he goes on building golden images of himself to be set up in the sight of men—while the heavenly watchers weep.

In fairness, it is not always the minister, initially, who places himself on the pedestal. The people place him there. The people adore him—well-nigh worship him. The people bear a large responsibility in the tempting of a minister to be proud of his pedestal position. And if the minister falls, if the star goes out, the people must share the blame.

Many people become so enamored of their minister that they begin to assume him infallible, as if he were some sort of god. They simply can't imagine him making a mistake. Much less can they believe that he has ever actually sinned.

Strangely enough, this state of things destroys a man's usefulness to many in his congregation in an unexpected way. Young people in trouble, for instance, may turn elsewhere for counsel, for they feel that a man so perfect could never stoop to understand their problems.

Could it be that there is too much man worship at the doors of churches on Sabbath mornings? Some of it is outright flattery. Some of it may be meant as sincere encouragement. But it may not be received that way. And the result of raising a man higher and higher each week may be spiritual dizziness—and a fall like Humpty Dumpty's.

The messenger of the Lord wrote: "It is not safe to speak in praise of persons or to exalt the ability of a minister of Christ. In the day of God, very many will be weighed in the balance and found wanting because of exaltation. I would warn my brethren and sisters never to flatter persons because of their ability, for they cannot bear it. Self is easily exalted, and, in consequence, persons lose their balance. . . . If you would have your souls clean from the blood of all men, never flatter, never praise the efforts of poor mortals; for it may prove their ruin. It is unsafe, by our words and actions, to exalt a brother or sister, however apparently humble may be their deportment. If they really possess the meek and lowly spirit which God so highly esteems, help them to retain it. This will not be done by censuring them nor by neglecting to properly appreciate their true worth. But there are few who can bear praise without being injured."—*Testimonies,* vol. 3, p. 185.

Applause stimulates. It intoxicates like wine. Human ears welcome flattery. But flattery puffs a man up. It spoils men. It turns men from God's approval. It unbalances them. It is Satan's work, Satan's merchandise, Satan's art. It is one of Satan's most successful devices to ruin souls. Flattery produces pride. And pride kills!

Next time you are tempted to flatter a minister at the door of the church or by way of a letter, think again. Do you really want to contribute to the ruin of the one you admire?

Pride is a deadly thing. And it is tricky. The proud man is often sure that he is humble. He is even proud of his humility. But once popularity has placed him on a pedestal, he feels an almost obsessive desire to protect his reputation. It is difficult for him ever to admit that he is wrong, for he rationalizes that he must maintain a high level of dignity and self-respect—for the sake of the work. The need to appear good in the eyes of others becomes pathological. The thought of being shown in an unfavorable light makes him sick. He goes on, suppressing any thought of danger, barely managing to conceal the crown on his head.

Just today it was reported that smallpox has finally been wiped out from the entire world—that no smallpox virus exists anywhere except in laboratories. I wish we could say that of the virus of pride. I wish I could believe that the affliction is extremely rare. I wish there were a vaccine to control it, to stamp it out. There is none but the blood of Jesus. And a proud man will not take the cure until he ceases to be proud.

Even if through the years I had not observed the disease in varying degrees, I still could not believe it is on the way out. It would be wishful and unjustified thinking to believe that pride has been conquered. Pride is at the very root of our problems. Pride is what cost Lucifer his place in heaven. And he and all his fallen angels are sworn to contaminate every man and woman possible with the virus. Ministers, because of their position in the spotlight, are peculiarly vulnerable. The tragedy is that some will fall.

No true preacher of Christ calls men to himself. No true representative of Christ ever invites or demands or accepts worship. Jonestown forever reminds us of the fearful results of man worship. Jonestown could never have happened if those poor, unhappy people had been looking at Jesus, worshiping and adoring Jesus, instead of Jim Jones.

But Jim Jones wanted it that way. He once threw the Bible on the floor and stamped on it, enraged. He said people were thinking of it instead of him. He didn't want the voice of the Bible to be heard. It would have reminded them, "Thou shalt have no other gods before me." Jim Jones bought Bibles for Jonestown. Yes, Bibles by the carton. To be used for toilet paper!

Jonestown was the ugly end of pride. But pride, in its beginning stages, is considered a respectable sin. Men are condemned for murder and theft and adultery. Men are jailed for some offenses. But has anyone ever been jailed for pride? Yet Jesus considered pride worse than adultery. Is there something wrong with our priorities?

Yes, for two reasons pride will not be easily stamped out. First, because Satan's entire staff of demons is promoting it. And second, it is still considered a respectable sin—as if we had some sort of silent agreement to overlook it.

There are some men and women who are happy only in a position, a profession, a career that gives them a sense of power over other people. They are happy as chairman of a large committee. They are happy leading a parade. They are happy with a baton in hand, conducting a great orchestra. They are happy sitting at a control board where they can push buttons and direct the activities of a large number of persons. And I do not mean to cast reflection upon any of these. There have been great and good men in these positions. I only ask, If a man is primarily seeking power over people, if that is his driving motive in life—is the ministry the place for him?

A friend of mine was asked to interview a young man, and I happened to be sitting in. The young man came in exuberant, fairly bursting with enthusiasm over his own talents. He had so much to contribute to the world. Where could he best show his talents to the fullest—in drama, in communications, or in the ministry? There was no indication whatever, on the outside at least, that the young man had any personal relationship with Christ. If it was there, it was well hidden. But he seemed very much in love with himself.

My friend turned to me. I suppose he thought that because I was there I should be included in the conversation in some way. He said, "I think I know what Mrs. Lloyd is thinking. I believe she is thinking, and I agree, that God is calling you into the ministry."

I'm sure that whatever I said was a little awkward, for my thoughts were completely opposite. I can't believe that God calls a man into the ministry just to give him a showplace for his talents. And I can't believe that God calls a man into the ministry who can't decide whether he wants to give himself to a life of pretense or to a life of preaching Christ.

No one is lonelier than the man whose pride has separated him from God, from real life, from genuine joy. No one is more miserable than the ambassador of Christ who has no personal relationship with the One he represents. Fellow ministers may see the need and try to help. They may speak tactfully of the need for humility. And he will agree. He will repeat after them, "God be merciful to me a sinner." But when a proud man speaks humble words that he does not feel, will it make him humble—or make him a hypocrite?

Said A. W. Tozer, "The worst feature about this whole thing is that it does no good to call attention to it. The bitter heart is not likely to recognize its own condition, and if the resentful man reads this he will smile smugly and think I mean someone else. In the meantime he will grow smaller and smaller trying to get bigger, and he will become more and more obscure trying to become known."—*Of God and Men*, p. 91.

And Ellen White wrote that God "regards all religious sham as an insult to Himself."—*S.D.A. Bible Commentary*, vol. 4, p. 1149.

From the same pen we read: "Satan watches every opportunity to crowd in some of his attributes. There is in the natural heart a tendency to be exalted or puffed up if success attends the efforts put forth. But self-exaltation can find no place in the work of God. Whatever your intelligence, however earnestly and zealously you may labor, unless you put away your own tendencies to pride, and submit to be guided by the Spirit of God, you will be on losing ground.

"Spiritual death in the soul is evidenced by spiritual pride and a crippled experience; those who have such an experience seldom make straight paths for their feet. If pride is nourished, the very qualities of the mind which grace, if received, would make a blessing, become contaminated. The very victories which would have been a savor of life unto life, if the glory had been given to God, become tarnished by self-glory. These may seem to be little things, unworthy of notice, but the seed thus scattered brings forth a sure harvest. It is these little sins, so common that they are often unnoticed, that Satan uses in his service."—*Ibid.*, vol. 6, p. 1080.

Spiritual pride, then spiritual death. And a subtle, almost indistinguishable line between!

I think of that fateful moment in heaven when pride in Lucifer's heart became sin. One moment sin did not exist. The next moment it did. One moment the entire universe was clean. The next moment it was contaminated. There may have been a time when Lucifer wanted a bigger drum with which to do good. I don't know. We are told that at first he did not understand the strange feelings inside him. He didn't know what was happening. But then he did, and he cherished those feelings still, and let them grow. The line had been crossed.

So it may be with a minister of the gospel. There is a relationship with Christ. But then prayer is pushed aside and the relationship is lost. And the change may not be immediately apparent from the platform.

God only knows the heart. Yet all of us, ministers and laymen, are more transparent to our fellow people than we think. Many a man's work has failed miserably to reach hearts because his whole effort is tainted with evident hypocrisy. The people see hypocrisy in a man—and weep over it—long before he sees it in himself.

But there's a happy side to the picture. It isn't all dark. Even though the disease of pride is rampant on this planet, many, many hearts are still untainted by it. All around the world there are workers for God who are beautifully humble, who are so fascinated with Jesus that they have no time or inclination to exalt self.

J. Wallace Hamilton was one of America's truly great preachers. But when his wife was asked what it was like to be married to a great preacher, she replied, "He doesn't know he's a great preacher."

You have known men like that. I have known men like that. There are thousands who have not bowed the knee to self, whose eyes are on Jesus only. They can hardly wait for the latter rain and the loud cry and for the Lord they love to return.

What would happen—what *could* happen—if all of us, every one of us, would throw away our pedestals and our stilts? Could it be that we might soon be aware of the latter rain if we would stand *under* the clouds instead of *above* them?

Without the Silly Stilts

Pastor Roger Bothwell had stopped at the local mortuary on an errand. On his way to the office he passed a room that was open, and he saw a young man standing pathetically beside a tiny casket. He asked the mortician about him. He was told that the little five-year-old son had been run over by a car, and the father was having a difficult time.

His errand completed, Pastor Bothwell walked back to the room. He stopped. He wanted so much to walk in and put his arm around that man and say, "Jesus Christ gives you back your son!"

But he hesitated. Then, he said, "I bowed my head and walked out without even trying. Why? Because if I said that and nothing happened, I would look like a fool. I didn't want to be personally embarrassed."

He continued, speaking to an audience in Portland, Oregon, "The problem is with ourselves. What *I* might look like. What *I* want people to think *I* am. So concerned for myself. I never even tried to help that man—and it might have been the greatest miracle of his life."

Pastor Bothwell spoke with deep feeling. "I hate to make hospital calls. I hate to visit nursing homes. I sit in my car, and I feel so guilty. I say I'm never going back. But I have to. It's my job. Yet I hate it. Those people hurting and dying because I haven't established the contact that would enable me to help them.

"I say, If this church has any need at all, it is the need for someone among us to be *humble enough* to walk up to a dead child and say, 'Arise in the name of Jesus'—and walk away and still be humble!

"And I pray there will be someone among us *humble enough,* so in love with Jesus and so little concerned about himself, that God will be able to do this through him. How it might finally awaken us! How it might drive some of the rest of us into a deeper prayer life, a deeper experience with Jesus!

"I really believe that if just one of us would lead, many would follow. We *can* do such a work. If you believe the Bible, you have to believe that we can. We stand tonight as a people so rich—oh, man, are we rich—and we are so poor. Oh, Lord, we're so poor! If only we would become a people of prayer!"

On another occasion he expressed the same concern—that we might become a people of prayer. But he said, "We aren't a people of prayer. We're a people of Vega-Links and Choplets!"

I have shared Roger Bothwell's impassioned appeal in some detail because it so moved me. It moved me for days. Why do we not see many miracles of healing among us? I know we are told that God limits His miracles of healing because Satan so easily counterfeits them. But I'm sure that isn't the only reason. Mark 16:18 clearly says of God's people, "They shall lay hands on the sick, and they shall recover." And we are told of a day coming, "Miracles will be wrought, the sick will be healed, and signs and wonders will follow the believers."—*The Great Controversy,* p. 612.

Someday. Why not now? We read that "the miracles of Christ for the afflicted and suffering were wrought by the power of God through the ministration of the angels "—*The Desire of Ages,* p. 143. Aren't the angels with us?

Well, here's a clue: "God cannot work through us miraculously while we are unconverted. It would spoil us; for we would take it as an evidence that we were perfect before Him. . . . Those who see Christ by living faith, those who abide in Him, will have power to work miracles for His glory."—Manuscript 169, 1902.

Humility again. It keeps cropping up!

I pondered the problem for days. But particularly I was fascinated by the question, Even if we are humble and even if our faith is right, does God expect His servants, on their own, to walk out on a limb and run the risk that nothing will happen, making us look like fools? Does He expect us to *initiate* bold moves—or does He clearly *tell us* what to do on every occasion?

I can certainly sympathize with the fear of personal embarrassment, the fear that nothing might happen in response to a bold move of faith. I don't suppose I fear anything more than being made conspicuous. I have called it timidity. But God may call it pride.

Early in 1978 I put my house up for sale. It was on the market for more than six months without a nibble. That was no problem, however, for conditions kept arising that would have made it difficult if not impossible to move at that time. Yet I kept telling people that God was going to sell it at just the right time, and I kept thanking God for what He was going to do. It seemed I was walking pretty far out on a limb, but I had no fear that God would let me down. And He didn't. When conditions changed so that I could move, the house sold in less than a week.

But walking up to one who is ill and saying "Jesus bids you rise and walk" is far different from selling a house. How would one know that the healing would be according to God's will? How would one know whether he was acting in faith or presumption?

When Peter healed the lame man at the temple gate, was he acting on his own or on specific instruction? Was he taking any risk? And what about Elijah on Mount Carmel? Was he sure of what would happen when he prayed? I spent a great deal of time searching the inspired words for the answers.

Peter was once a proud man. He stepped out once—on the water. And his pride got soaking wet. But Peter at Pentecost, I found, was modest and self-distrustful. I found no evidence that he was specifically instructed to heal the cripple. But Peter was filled by the Spirit, undoubtedly led by the Spirit. And his eyes were on Jesus. I found these words: "Of the disciples after the transfiguration of Christ, it is written that at the close of that wonderful scene, 'they saw no man, save Jesus only.' 'Jesus only'—in these words is contained the secret of the life and power that marked the history of the early church."—*The Acts of the Apostles*, p. 64.

And the secret is also right in the book of Acts, in the words spoken by Peter and John to their accusers. Listen to this: "Whether it be right in the sight of God to hearken unto you more than unto God, judge ye. For we *cannot but speak* the things which we have seen and heard." Acts 4:19, 20.

Peter and John didn't have to clench their fists and whip up their courage and say to each other, "Now we've got to be brave. We've got to be bold and fearless." Nor were they inwardly trembling with fear of possible embarrassment when they healed the cripple. "We *cannot but speak* the things which we have seen and heard." They *couldn't help speaking* about Jesus. They were so in love with Jesus, they were so filled with the Spirit that they *couldn't help but be bold and fearless*. Their relationship with Jesus was such that they *couldn't help but heal the cripple*. They were only doing what now came naturally!

But what about Elijah? If any man ever made bold moves, it was Elijah. Did he take risks? I checked through to find out.

Interestingly, I found no record that Elijah was specifically instructed to call the widow's son to life. Some say he simply administered artificial respiration. Whether it was a resurrection or a resuscitation or a healing does not matter—it was a miracle. But the miracle was not done publicly. It was done in the privacy of Elijah's room, where his prayer was heard by God alone. Did he know that his prayer would be answered?

But with the possible exception of that one incident, Elijah seems to have been specifically instructed all the way. His bold acts were not presumption. Nor was he risking embarrassment by walking out too far and having nothing happen.

It is true that Elijah was deeply concerned about conditions in Israel. It is true that he prayed that God would send judgments upon the people if necessary to awaken them. But he did not ask to be God's messenger. He was specifically sent to Ahab. His message was God's message.

Elijah was sent to the brook Cherith and told that the ravens would feed him there. He was told to go to Zarephath and that a widow there would provide for him. He was instructed to go back to Ahab, and he was told that God would send rain. And apparently everything he did in the confrontation atop Mount Carmel was at God's instruction, for we read, "Unashamed, unterrified, the prophet stands before the multitude, fully aware of his commission to execute the divine command."—*Prophets and Kings*, p. 147.

I don't believe Elijah was one bit fearful that the fire would not come down. And we read that "Elijah is directed by the Lord to destroy these false teachers."—*Ibid.*, p. 154.

But now wait. The rain. God had told Elijah He would send rain. And the prophet told Ahab to get ready for it. But now it wasn't so easy. He retired alone, back to the top of Carmel, to pray. And he sent his servant to watch for evidence of the answer. And what happened?

"The servant watched while Elijah prayed. Six times he returned from the watch, saying, There is nothing, no cloud, no sign of rain. But the prophet did not give up in discouragement. He kept reviewing his life, to see where he had failed to honor God, he confessed his sins, and thus continued to afflict his soul before God, while watching for a token that his prayer was answered. As he searched his heart, he seemed to be less and less, both in his own estimation and in the sight of God. It seemed to him that he was nothing, and that God was everything; and when he reached the point of renouncing self, while he clung to the Saviour as his only strength and righteousness, the answer came. The servant appeared, and said, 'Behold, there ariseth a little cloud out of the sea, like man's hand.' "—Ellen G. White Comments, *S.D.A. Bible Commentary*, vol. 2, p. 1035.

We ought to read that paragraph over and over until we are never unaware of it. We think of Elijah as a man of power. But "as he searched his heart, he seemed to be less and less, both in his own estimation and in the sight of God. It seemed to him that he was nothing, and that God was everything." How many of us pray like that—and mean it? Is it possible that we have focused too much on Elijah's power—

which wasn't his at all—and not enough on his relationship with his Lord? Is it any wonder that God could use him?

"Elijah humbled himself until he was in a condition where he would not take the glory to himself. This is the condition upon which the Lord hears prayer, for then we shall give the praise to Him. The custom of offering praise to men is one that results in great evil. One praises another, and thus men are led to feel that glory and honor belong to them. When you exalt man, you lay a snare for his soul, and do just as Satan would have you. You should praise God with all your heart, soul, might, mind, and strength; for God alone is worthy to be glorified."—*Ibid.*, vol. 2, p. 1035.

Elijah—symbol of power! But evidently there is more to the story when we search it out. "The success of the ministry of Elijah was not due to any inherited qualities he possessed, but to the submission of himself to the Holy Spirit, which was given to him as it will be given to all who exercise living faith in God. In his imperfection man has the privilege of linking himself up with God through Jesus Christ."—*Ibid.*, p. 1037.

You and I, too, can link up with Jesus as did Elijah. Then why don't we?

"Oh, how many have fallen because they trusted in their profession for salvation! How many are lost by their effort to keep up a name! If one has the reputation of being a successful evangelist, a gifted preacher, a man of prayer, a man of faith, a man of special devotion, there is positive danger that he will make shipwreck of faith when tried by the little tests that God suffers to come. Often his great effort will be to maintain his reputation.

"He who lives in the fear that others do not appreciate his value is losing sight of Him who alone makes us worthy of glorifying God. . . . All the work done, however excellent it may appear to be, is worthless if not done in the love of Jesus. One may go through the whole round of religious activity, and yet, unless Christ is woven into all that he says and does, he will work for his own glory."—*Ibid.*, vol. 7, p. 958.

If power and reputation had been the goal of Elijah, would the fire have come down? Would he ever have seen that little cloud? Would God have sent him to Carmel in the first place?

There are three reasons God could use Elijah. He was a man of prayer. He was a man of great faith. He was a man of remarkable and rare humility.

So our problem today is apparently not that we haven't the courage, the boldness, to walk out on a limb for God. He may not even *expect* us to do that. The problem, rather, is this: Why doesn't God *instruct us, command us, tell us* to do great things for Him? Why *doesn't* He? And why *can't* He? He *could* if we were a people of prayer. He *could* if we had great faith. And great faith would come naturally with a life of prayer. A relationship with Jesus is a life of miracles all the way—miracles *for* us. Then why not miracles *through* us?

Now comes the hard part. We aren't humble enough. God doesn't dare to use us as He used Elijah until we are *willing*, as Elijah was willing, *to be nothing*.

Remember how Elijah ran in front of Ahab's carriage that rainy night, so that the king could find his way down the mountain? How many of us would be willing, in a driving rain, to run down Howell Mountain—down the slippery miles between Pacific Union College and Saint Helena—so that someone, maybe an enemy, could find his way? Wouldn't we think that a little beneath us? Wouldn't we, like the disciples on that last Thursday night, think it was something for someone else to do? But Jesus would do it!

If only we would come down from our stilts of self-exaltation and let the Lord use us as He so wants to use us!

By the way, Elijah, being human, may have been as reluctant as we to take a risk—to walk out on a limb and take the chance that nothing would happen. I feel sure he wouldn't want to end up looking like a fool any more than we. But the only time he ended up looking bad was when he stopped praying, lost his faith, and set out on a wild journey with no command whatever—without receiving, or even asking, instruction. That's when he came nearest to looking like a fool. Yet God loved His tired servant then as much as ever. And He loves us.

But think what would have happened if Elijah *had* asked God what to do on that rainy night? God, we are told, would have sent terrible judgment on Jezebel. And Elijah would have continued to be, under God, the hero of Carmel—not a fleeing, frightened refugee on a stormy night.

In the final days just ahead of us God's servants will walk farther out on limbs, take greater apparent risks, than ever before. They will make bold and brave moves. Qualified not by literary training but by the Spirit of God, they will speak with power. Thousands upon thousands will listen—to words such as they have never heard before. God's men will speak words that they are constrained to speak—because the divine impulse is strong upon them. God will put truth into their hearts, and how could they remain silent except at the peril of their souls? Like Peter and John, how could they help but speak what they have seen and heard? And they won't be clenching their fists to drum up courage to speak. They will be doing only what comes naturally for a man linked up with Christ and filled with His Spirit. (See *The Great Controversy*, pp. 606-612.)

But the pedestal people will have no part in it. For either they will have joined the enemy camp, where pedestals and popularity and boasted power block the vision and blind the eyes of those who move steadily toward the final precipice—or they will have left their pedestals and their stilts and their crutches of silly pride behind, to be firewood for the final day. They will need them no more. For they will have learned that a man on bended knee, and in Calvary's light, can see farther and higher and far more clearly than one standing shakily atop his phony props of pride!

The Sinner's Declaration

Did you ever read "The Sinners Declaration of Independence"? Here it is—with the permission of an author who chooses to remain anonymous:

"God sent me a communication today—some things He wanted me to do. But I looked it over and found it conflicted with the program I have already worked out. I noticed, too, that what He requested was nothing new or fresh—very similar to the rest of His communications, all marked URGENT.

"So it didn't bother me at all to put His program on a dusty shelf. Mine is working fine. And it's better to be successful with my own plan than to flounder with His.

"Of course if He sends me something I like sometime—though that is highly unlikely—I can always pick it up and make use of it. But I don't want to be a victim of the system. I want to feel I am in command.

"You see, I've been a successful sinner for a number of years now—long enough to reach some independent conclusions. I think every sinner should work out his own declaration of independence and stick to it. He should be his own man.

"I became a better sinner when I realized that I don't have to stay where I am. There are a number of other jobs I can do well. I'm not dependent on God for my bread and butter.

"For instance, I'm a scientist. I'm a computer man. An engineer. I'm deep into technology. If God makes it too uncomfortable for me on this planet, there are plenty more. They'll need a computer man out there in this space colony that's in the works. Or I could establish a community on the moon. Jupiter has always interested me. It will take a good engineer to make it habitable. And I don't have to stop with this solar system. Or even with this galaxy.

"I have a lot more self-respect now that I've settled this in my mind. I'm just more comfortable if I'm not worrying about being banished to the flames someday for making a wrong move.

"I have to have an atmosphere where I can create and innovate. I have to be myself. Motivated. Independent. In charge. Otherwise it isn't worth it!

" 'Hello! . . . Who? . . . Jupiter? . . . Tomorrow morning? . . . I need a little more time than that. . . . I guess I'm stuck here for a few years yet. . . .'

"Imagine! God said I was cocky!"

Dismantling the Float

You may have heard the classic story of the frog who wanted to spend the winter in Florida. He had no way to get there, but he had a couple of friends in the goose family who were well equipped for air flight. So the frog managed to find a stout piece of string. He persuaded each of his geese friends to take hold of an end, and he, with his strong jaws, took firm hold of the string in the middle. They were on their way.

The flight was proceeding well, when a spectator on the ground looked up and saw what was happening. He was so astonished and so moved with admiration that he said aloud, "Who in the world invented that idea?" And the frog heard him. He simply couldn't resist the impulse to take full credit for the performance; so he opened his mouth to say "I." And that was the end of the frog!

There's one thing about a parade. It always comes to an end. And then there's nothing to do but dismantle the float and throw away the wilted flowers. Then appear the unfinished boards and poles beneath, with all their flaws. The glamour has slipped away.

A proud man doesn't want his float dismantled. He doesn't want the bubble pricked. He doesn't want his balloon deflated. It's a time of embarrassment. But he can't avoid it. Every parade, sooner or later, comes to a grinding halt. The game is up. And all the world knows.

Sometimes it happens very suddenly and without warning.

The most powerful man in the world rode proudly, and he thought securely, in a Dallas motorcade. A few hours later John Kennedy was only a memory.

That moment of truth comes to all men—the great and good and the notoriously bad. God decides which is which.

In the days of Xerxes the Great, king of Medo-Persia, there lived a man high in the royal court who dearly loved a parade. His name was Haman. He loved to be led through the streets at the head of the procession. The only thing wrong was that one man refused to worship him. That bothered him. That irritated him. That spoiled his day every time it happened. It festered in his mind until he built a gallows on which to hang the hated Mordecai.

But it didn't work out quite that way. One night the king couldn't sleep, and he asked his aides to read to him from the records. Among other things they read that Mordecai had once saved the king's life by warning of a plot to kill him. What had been done to honor him? Nothing. The king determined to remedy this oversight.

The next morning Haman came to ask the king to hang Mordecai on the gallows he had prepared. But before he could make his request, the king asked, "What shall we do for a man that I would like to honor?" Haman was sure that he himself must be the one the king wished to honor; so here was his chance. He suggested that the man be dressed in the king's robe with the king's crown on his head, and placed on the king's horse. Then someone high in the court should lead him through the streets proclaiming, "This is the man the king wishes to honor." This would be it! This would be the ultimate!

And the king said, "That's a good idea, Haman. The man is Mordecai. You take care of it. Do as you have suggested. Go and lead him through the streets in a big parade."

So Haman led the hated man who wouldn't worship him through the streets—and fumed every minute. What a dismantling of his pride! What humiliation! If ever it rained on anybody's parade, it rained on Haman's. It wasn't even *his* parade!

As you recall, things went from bad to intolerable. And

Haman ended up on the gallows he had built for Mordecai!

It's an embarrassing thing to have to look up at those you've looked down on. There's an old but true story that makes the point, without the tragedy of Haman's experience. It's about two fine Boston gentlemen who were hanging onto the straps of a trolley one afternoon. Below them were seated two deaf mutes, conversing in sign language.

One of the straphangers whispered to his friend, "I'm curious about something." Then he took a note pad from his pocket and wrote, "Can you write?" He handed it to one of the deaf-mutes, who studied it carefully. The he slowly drew from his pocket an elegant, expensive fountain pen. It was the color of emerald and trimmed in gold. And then, with a grand flourish, he wrote a few words on the note pad and handed it back to the gentlemen who were standing.

Imagine their chagrin as they read, in exquisite penmanship, "Can you read?"

The Lord's messenger wrote, "What is justification by faith? It is the work of God in laying the glory of man in the dust, and doing for man that which it is not in his power to do for himself."—*Testimonies to Ministers*, p. 456.

I cannot understand all the confusion about righteousness by faith when there is such a simple, clear, beautiful, and fully adequate inspired definition. And yet I *can* understand it. Proud hearts do not *want* their glory laid in the dust. They are not willing to admit there is anything they cannot do for themselves. The experience of righteousness by faith calls for a surrender that the proud man is not willing to make. And so there will always be controversy about it, unfortunately—until we enter a land where proud hearts are excluded.

If only we could realize that having our glory laid in the dust is not the end of the world. Rock bottom is not such a bad place to be. It is sometimes the only place to get started right. Falling on our faces, having our floats unceremoniously dismantled while others watch, having the balloon popped, failing miserably again and again, realizing that there is absolutely nothing we can do to lift ourselves an inch, coming to the end of our hope—any or all of these could be the best thing that ever happened to us. They are God's opportunity. Then, at last, we may be willing to let God take over and do for us what we can't do for ourselves!

One day the glory of man will all be blown away in the wind. Why not let the Holy Spirit blow it away now? Why not get down on our knees and dismantle the float ourselves, as Elijah did, before God has to do it for us?

A friend of mine was angry, very angry. Her husband was making unreasonable demands. He was unfair. He was accusing her falsely, saying she was lazy, expecting a spotless house when she was not well. He was asking too much. He was wrong. She knew he was wrong. And she was right. She was always right.

The fury built up until she couldn't stand it. Something terrible was going to happen to her. A nervous breakdown. Something. And she burst out, almost shouting, "Dear God, You have to do something for me right now!"

Immediately a quiet voice said clearly, "Humble yourself and do your work."

She told me the experience one evening as she was visiting. And then she said, "You see, I told you this for a reason. I'm building up to a question. What does it mean to humble yourself? And she added, "I know I was right."

Oh, friend, to humble yourself means to say, "I was wrong." It means to say, "I'm to blame. No one else. Me." It means to get down on your knees and pray, "God be merciful to me a sinner." Even if you're right? Yes, even if you're right. Even if you are only a little bit wrong and the other person is a hundred times more wrong than you? Yes. Does it mean to confess your little bit of wrong even if the other person does not admit any of his hundred-times-greater wrong? Yes.

This is the inspired word: "If there is any point on which you have committed one wrong, although he may have committed one hundred, take that which you have done out of the way and open the way for him to come back again. Perhaps that was the very thing that was keeping a soul away. In your humility, confess your one wrong, and perhaps it may touch him and lead him with weeping to confess his hundred wrongs, and to take them out of the way."—*Our High Calling,* p. 178.

And if it doesn't work, if the other person accepts your confession as if yours were all the guilt and his all the innocence, don't lose your balance. Don't let it affect your relationship with Jesus. pray for the unrelenting one. But pray more for yourself that your own heart may be right, realizing that *the other person's problem* is between him and his God. It can't keep you out of heaven. But *yours* can!

It is not easy to say, "I was wrong." It is not easy to say, "I'm to blame." Yet pride needs nothing so much as a fall. Our stupid parades need nothing so much as a drenching, wilting rain that will cut us down to size.

We need so desperately to be linked up with Jesus. But union with Jesus "costs us something. It is a relation of utter dependence to be entered into by a proud being."—Ellen G. White Comments, *S.D.A. Bible Commentary,* vol. 5, p. 1144.

Is it any wonder that righteousness by faith is accepted as a theory, as a topic for debate, but resisted as a life? The surrender it requires is difficult, so difficult, for the proud heart. Because so long as a man is totally absorbed with the wonder of what he is doing himself, he is not ready for the wonder of what *God* can do!

"Laying the glory of man in the dust, and doing for man that which it is not in his power to do for himself." To the humble it is a golden secret. It is life in place of death. It is joy that cannot be described. It is victory in place of defeat. It is Jesus where self used to be!

But to the proud man it is an intolerable burden that he will never touch until he quits his pride. No wonder it is controversial. It will always be—so long as one proud heart is left!

Jesus had come home—home to Nazareth. And on Sabbath morning He made His way to the meetinghouse—just as He always had before He left the carpenter shop and went hiking around the country with his little group of disciples, working miracles. What would He be like now? What would He do today? Would He work any of those miracles here—at home?

The scroll of the prophet Isaiah was handed to Him. He unrolled it and began to read:

"The Spirit of the Lord is on me, because he has anointed me to preach good news to the poor. He has sent me to proclaim freedom for the prisoners and recovery of sight for the blind, to release the oppressed, to proclaim the year of the Lord's favor." Luke 4:18, 19, N.I.V.

How beautifully He read—just as He always had. His neighbors were so proud of Him.

But wait! Was He saying that Isaiah was talking about *Him*? Was He claiming to be the Messiah? The Messiah would descend in a cloud over the temple. No one would know where He came from. But there was no mystery about where Jesus came from. They knew who He was. He was Joseph's son. Jesus had gone too far. His disciples had turned His head. And they dragged Him out to a cliff, ready to throw Him over. They would have—if angels had not intervened.

But what a great meeting it *could have been* that day! There before them had stood the Saviour of the world. There before them had stood the One sent to free the captives, to give sight to the blind. Their chains of unbelief could have dropped away. They could have been changed forever. What a day it could have been!

And what a day it *could be* for us, for you and me—now! Jesus still is waiting with good news for the poor who think they are rich. He still stands ready to open the eyes that have not been willing to see. *Our* stubborn chains, too, could fall away at His word. Every prisoner of pride could be set free forever!

Why are we so reluctant to accept the wonder of it all?

God Believes in Privacy

It was back in 1973 that *Time* magazine reported the invention and testing of a device it called the antidream machine. No larger than a pack of cigarettes, it uses electrodes and measures brainwaves in order to gauge a person's level of concentration. If his mind begins to wander, a tone sounds and jolts him from his reverie. If he keeps on daydreaming, another alarm goes off—and this one notifies his boss, his teacher, or some Big Brother who can take matters in hand.

This little instrument was designed by scientist Karel Montor, and was first tested on midshipmen volunteers at the U.S. Naval Academy. When their minds strayed and they began to think about their girl friends or their next leave—bong! They were found out. The machine, it is said, like the fear of being hanged, has a wonderful power to concentrate the mind. Think of how many accidents could be avoided if the device were hooked up to bus drivers or truck drivers or airline pilots—air-traffic controllers too!

I haven't heard anything more about this little device. I don't know whether it was ever put into actual use anywhere or not. But *Time* rightly concluded that the right to daydream—the right to pay attention or not pay attention—should be rigidly respected and even fought for if necessary. A machine that could banish idle reveries would be a nightmare!

Another device however—one that comes very close to revealing a man's thoughts—has in recent years come into quite extensive use. It is the psychological stress evaluator—or PSE for short. It is designed to test a man's truthfulness or lack of truthfulness. And it seems to be doing it with remarkable accuracy.

The PSE differs considerably from the traditional polygraph—or lie detector, as it is called. The polygraph detects deception by recording and measuring various bodily functions—the heartbeat, the blood pressure, the respiration rate. These tend to be affected when a person attempts to lie or deceive.

But now we know that the human voice, too, is affected by the attempt to deceive. Voices not only lie—they betray that they are lying.

You see, the human voice consists of more than the sound we hear, the frequencies we hear. The voice also has an inaudible frequency, known as a microtremor. Any attempt to deceive causes tension in the human body, and that tension results in a suppression of the microtremors in the voice box. *We* cannot hear that stress or measure it. But the PSE can. And it records it on a strip of electrocardiograph paper.

Another difference in the two lie-detection instruments is that the PSE does not require a person to submit to an interview and be hooked up to a machine. It uses the recorded voice. This means that any statement made on radio or TV or in any public speech that is recorded can be put into the machine and tested. It is no wonder that the PSE is controversial, that VIPs hate it, and that there is no standing in line to see how they score. Anything a man says, if it gets on tape, could wind up on a PSE somewhere!

Unquestionably our right to the exclusive ownership of our thoughts is being threatened in more ways than one.

We have a God, however, who believes in the right of privacy. True, He can read our thoughts. He is aware of even our daydreams. He knows when we are proud without anyone tattling or anyone confessing. Yet God has set certain limits on Himself. He has given us the right to think without outside control—and the right to decide without coercion. He will never invade the sacred precincts of the soul where a man decides. He waits at the door. He calls. He pleads. But

He will not enter uninvited. Nor will He allow anyone else to enter. Satan would like to enter. There are churches and cults and governments that would like to enter. But God says to the assembled universe, "Stand back! The soul must be free!"

Can you imagine Jesus, on a visit to Bethany, secretly opening Mary's mail to see if she was really going straight? Or Martha's—to see how much she was spending on entertaining? Holding the envelope up to the light—or steaming open the flaps? No. Jesus is not like that!

Jesus knew the thoughts of Judas. He knew when he was proud. But can you imagine Him hounding Judas about it? Or equipping him with a device that would go "bong" whenever his thoughts took a wrong road? No. Jesus knew. Jesus prayed and wept and waited. But He respected the privacy of Judas, his right to think and to choose. He never exposed him till the very end!

How tenderly our Lord spares us from embarrassment, from public exposure, long after He sees where pride is leading us. It is only rarely that, for our good, He exposes our thoughts to public view!

The African baobab is a most unusual tree. It looks as if it were growing upside down. The legend is that the baobab was once the largest and most beautiful tree in Africa. Its foliage was green and lustrous. It grew in perfect symmetry, with lofty and noble branches. But it began to boast of its beauty. And the Creator, in order to humble it, uprooted the proud baobab and thrust its branches into the ground, leaving its roots sticking up awkwardly in the air. And so, to this day, the baobab appears to be growing upside down.

God hasn't turned us upside down yet. Maybe He will have to someday. But in the meantime it's still our parade. God's Watergate investigation is well out of our hearing. There are no bugs for our thoughts. No antipride machine. And there is no living prophet around to make us uncomfortable.

Having a living prophet on the job can be very disturbing. Suddenly appearing like Nathan. Capturing our attention and stirring our ire with a story. And then saying, "Thou art the man."

Is it possible that thousands are secretly glad that we have no living prophet among us today? And could it be that we take advantage of that fact? Would a lot of things be different if we knew that most any day we personally might receive a message from the Lord—the envelope addressed in the familiar handwriting of His messenger? Do we take advantage, to our hurt, of the fact that Ellen White no longer addresses our councils or stands up in our committees—or sends letters that cross the ocean to arrive at the precise moment they are needed? Do we feel secure, too secure, in the thought that the boasting of our inner souls will never be opened to the gaze of others?

We have the Scriptures. We have the books. It is not difficult to discover what God thinks of our foolish pride. But it is so easy to escape the written words. God does not take us by the arm and sit us down and turn the pages for us. And the proceedings of Heaven's court are not wired into our ears. The soul is still free!

But the voice we hear calling is that of the One who was not too proud to die for us. The hands reaching out in invitation are wounded hands. And when we respond, all heaven sings!

Gabriel Stands By

It is a satisfying thing to look up to something. Seeing it steady and strong. Like looking up into the heavens at night, the stars all in their places. Knowing that all is right with God's universe.

There is nothing more unsettling than to see a star drop down across the horizon into oblivion. A star of the human variety, I mean. But God said it would happen.

"At that time the gold will be separated from the dross. True godliness will be clearly distinguished from the appearance and tinsel of it. Many a star that we have admired for its brilliance will then go out in darkness."—*Prophets and Kings,* p. 188.

Here and there a light whose brilliance has shone around the world, admired by multitudes, will go out. A veteran warrior will fall, a victim of his own indiscretion. A champion of truth will turn to the propaganda of error. A name will drop out of the papers you read on Friday evening and be seen no more. And it could be someone you know, someone to whom you thought it could never happen.

It is not only a comfortable thing, but a good thing, to have confidence in others, especially in the leadership of the church. There is nothing more deadly than the spirit of criticism. And it does its cruelest work upon the individual who indulges in it. Never should the influence of a minister of the gospel be weakened by careless words of subtle implications that fray the edges of a man's reputation or his standing before others. If your confidence is shaken, keep it to yourself. God will right every wrong in His own way. He has not committed that work to you or me.

But never let your confidence in God be measured by your confidence in men. Never equate your certainty that the movement will go through with your uncertain certainty that men will go through. They are not one and the same thing. Settle it now that you will never allow your confidence in God and His message to be dependent upon the spiritual integrity of any one man or group of men. For at least a few of those stars will go out. And if we have no other light, how dark will be the darkness!

"In the last solemn work a few great men will be engaged. They are self-sufficient, independent of God, and he cannot use them."—*Testimonies,* vol. 5, p. 80.

If that is true, and of course it is, then why should we covet greatness—as the world calls greatness? "A great name among men," we are told, "is as letters traced in sand."—*Ibid.,* p. 579.

"God can teach you more in one moment by His Holy Spirit than you could learn from the great men of the earth."—*Testimonies to Ministers,* p. 119.

"God will work a work in our day that but few anticipate. He will raise up and exalt among us those who are taught rather by the unction of His Spirit than by the outward training of scientific institutions. These facilities are not to be despised or condemned; they are ordained of God, but they can furnish only the exterior qualifications. God will manifest that He is not dependent on learned, self-important mortals."—*Testimonies,* vol. 5, p. 82.

The trouble with learning is the self-importance that seems to follow it like a shadow.

Fritz Guy has written a refreshing article in which he says, "One of our illusions is the importance we attach to personal or professional status, leading to inappropriate feelings of superiority or inferiority." And he continues, "In the academic community of the church (in which I have served happily for more than 12 years) there are many kinds of status-consciousness. We have academic rank, which is really a professorial caste system (except that it allows for some upward mobility): first instructor, then assistant professor, then associate professor, then professor, and even distinguished professor. And we have advanced degrees—suggesting that a person with a Ph.D. is somehow better than those poor benighted souls who cannot claim those magic letters. But the fact remains that the tenured professor with an Ivy League Ph.D., just like the instructor with a State-college B.A.—indeed, just like the person who quit school in the tenth grade—is a plain, ordinary servant. When I became a college dean, I discovered that I was as capable of talking nonsense as before; the difference was that when I was a lowly instructor no one took me seriously, but when I was a dean, people believed what I said, because I said it."—*Adventist Review,* Nov. 16, 1978.

Every servant of God, whatever his academic background, has an incomparable privilege: "All who engage in ministry are God's helping hand. They are co-workers with the angels; rather, they are the human agencies through whom the angels accomplish their mission. Angels speak through their voices, and work by their hands. And the human workers, co-operating with heavenly agencies, have the benefit of their education and experience. As a means of education, what 'university course' can equal this?"—*Education,* p. 271.

What a privilege we have! The companionship of angels! And the lovely Jesus as our perfect Pattern. We are told concerning Him, "The best circles of human society would have courted him, had he condescended to accept their favor, but he desired not the applause of men, but moved independent of all human influence. Wealth, position, worldly rank in all its varieties and distinctions of human greatness, was all but so many degrees of littleness to him who had left the honor and glory of heaven, and who possessed no earthly splendor, indulged in no luxury, and displayed no adornment but humility."—Ellen G. White, *Review and Herald,* Dec. 22, 1891.

Why do the stars go out? Why do they turn their backs on all that could be theirs?

Some go out because they have not resisted sensual temptation. And some go out because they "hold that the opinions of a few conceited philosophers, so called, are more to be trusted than the truth of the Bible, or the testimonies of the Holy Spirit. Such a faith as that of Paul, Peter, or John is considered old-fashioned, and insufferable at the present day. It is pronounced absurd, mystical, and unworthy of an intelligent mind. God has shown me that these men are . . . to prove a scourge to our people."—*Testimonies,* vol. 5, p. 79.

But these are the exception. Most of the stars that go out will cease to shine for the same reason that Lucifer no longer stands by the throne—*pride!*

The stars go out because, like Lucifer, they trip over their own brilliance.

The stars go out because they want a bigger showplace for their unique talents—and they think they see such an opportunity on the outside.

The stars go out because they find in the service of God no glory for themselves. They have asked, "What's in it for me?" And they have answered, "Not enough."

The stars go out because they have mistaken their own dynamic personality for the power of the Spirit of God.

The stars go out because they are people-users. They have regarded every other person as either a stepping-stone or an obstacle to their own success. They have had time for only those persons who could help them up the ladder. They have loved people in theory but not in practice, in general but not in particular. And while the hungry sheep have crowded about, they have been busy preparing a banquet spread for themselves.

The stars go out because they are troubled at any suggestion that the Spirit of God works through anyone but themselves. The success of others makes them unhappy. If God has any miracles to work, they don't want another man to be the chosen channel. Yet can God work miracles through a man who would surely take the glory to himself? Can God work through a man who, unlike Jesus, would try to get all the miracles into prime time so that the most could witness them?

The stars go out because "by uniting with the world and partaking of its spirit, they have come to view matters in nearly the same light; and when the test is brought, they are prepared to choose the easy, popular side."—*The Great Controversy,* p. 608.

The stars go out because they desire God's power but not His character.

The stars go out because they are not in love with Jesus!

It doesn't happen all at once. It happens little by little, day by day, decision by decision, word by word, and thought by thought. Little by little a man changes, and his face begins to show it. Either it reflects more and more the countenance of the lovely Jesus. Or it betrays the marks of spiritual decay. Little by little a man's voice is changed too. It is changed by hours of prayer. Or it is changed by harsh and cutting words, by argument and debate. It begins to lose its power.

True, there may be a leftover momentum from the days when the power was there. An engine may break loose and begin to move downgrade. It gains speed. There is fantastic momentum. Looking on, you may say, "What power!"

No, friend. It isn't power! It's only the pull of gravity. And sooner or later—at the bottom of the grade—the engine will come to a crashing halt—and people will be hurt.

Is it possible that much that we call spiritual power is only the forced and practiced momentum of personality—and that one day we shall see that what we thought was the work of the Holy Spirit was only the pull of gravity?

A man may hide for a time what is going on inside. But not for long. His family begins to see it. Then his friends. And finally the day comes when suddenly a bright light has gone out. And thousands are stunned!

Such a man for years may carry a crushing load of guilt. But he is too proud to repent. Repentance is for other people. To admit his guilt, to ask forgiveness, would destroy his image. People would not respect him, he thinks, if he called his sins by the right name. Repentance is too rough for the proud heart!

It must be a heart-wrenching experience to watch a star going out. And worse still to see one already blackened and burned, its light gone out forever!

The story of D. M. Canright is one of the saddest, most

tragic stories ever told. Thousands know him only as a bitter opponent of Seventh-day Adventists. They know little of the real story.

Dudley M. Canright was a Seventh-day Adventist for twenty-eight years and an ordained minister of the church for twenty-two years. He was known as a successful evangelist.

But those years were checkered with periods of doubt and depression. Marked weaknesses of character appeared, with behavior that signaled danger. He was much admired and praised by those who heard him and was at his best in hot debate. Debating was a common practice in the nineteenth century, and Adventist ministers were often challenged to debate.

On the night following one of these debates, in which Canright had been successful, George I. Butler, president of the Iowa Conference, shared a room with the young Canright, probably in a hotel. Pastor Butler was astounded to learn that the young man was under the powerful temptation to give up religion, renounce his belief in the Scriptures, and become an out-and-out infidel. All night long the two men talked and prayed. Neither slept. The next morning Canright seemed to be all right and again threw himself zealously into the work.

He had obsessive desire, however, to be a great man. On one occasion, late one night after a meeting, he was talking with D. W. Reavis. He asked for a criticism of his presentation that evening. Reavis had none. He confessed that he had been carried away with the subject. They sat in silence for a time. Then suddenly Canright sprang to his feet and said, "D. W., I believe I could become a great man were it not for our unpopular message."

The young man also dreamed of becoming president of the General Conference when James White should retire. Or he thought he would be happy as president of the Michigan Conference. Attending the Michigan camp meeting in 1886, he remarked to a cousin of his, "If I am not elected president of this Conference at this meeting I am not going to preach for them anymore."

But George I. Butler was elected.

In the 1880s Canright's perilous position was shown to Ellen White in a dream. She saw him on a strong and sturdy ship sailing rough waters. He was determined to board another ship. The captain warned him that the other ship was a deceptive craft, its timbers worm-eaten, and it would never make the harbor. But he was determined to take it.

The warning was passed on to Canright. But not long after that he left the Adventist Church and boarded the phantom ship that seemed, to him, to hold more promise. And with that decision both his happiness and his power forever left him.

It was in 1903 that D. W. Reavis, a lifelong friend, invited Canright to attend a meeting of Adventist workers in Battle Creek. The now outspoken opponent of Adventists came and was delighted to be with his former associates again. He told Reavis that he wished the past could be blotted out and that he was back in the work just as he was at the beginning.

"I tried," says Reavis, "to get him to say to the workers there assembled just what he had said to me, assuring him that they would be glad to forgive all and to take him back in full confidence. I never heard any one weep and moan in such deep contrition as that once leading light in our message did. It was heartbreaking even to hear him. He said he wished he could come back to the fold as I suggested, but after long, heartbreaking moans and weeping, he said: 'I would be glad to come back, but I can't! It's too late! I am forever gone! Gone!' As he wept on my shoulder, he thanked me for all I had tried to do to save him from that sad hour. He said, 'D. W., whatever you do, don't ever fight the message.'"

Again and again, on varied occasions, he repeated the heartrending words, "It's too late.!"

Carrie Johnson, many years after Canright's death, wrote a book about him—*I Was Canright's Secretary*. It is not the critical, biased sort of book you might expect. Rather, it is the sympathetic, pitiful story of a lost man who loved Adventists and the Adventist message to his death but had no power to come back. I urge you to read the book!

The author includes in the book, of course, her own experience when as a student in Battle Creek she served as secretary to the then shabby, broken man. Here is an excerpt that is just a sample of what she observed:

"From day to day Mr. Canright labored on his books. He had only a little work to do to complete his book *The Lord's Day*. At the same time he was revising the introductory material for a new printing of *Seventh-day Adventism Renounced*.... But after his trip to Lincoln his main bookwork was the dictating of the chapters for the volume which he entitled *Life of Mrs. E. G. White*. This was not a biography, as the title might suggest, but an attack on Mrs. White and an attempt to 'expose' her.

"When he was dictating personal letters, I usually sat opposite his desk. At such times he was calm, composed, and had a note of assurance in his voice. Occasionally he would come to some point in his dictating in which he referred to Mrs. White. Strange as it may seem, his references, made almost inadvertently it seemed, were often favorable. But when he turned to his work on the *Life of Mrs. E. G. White*, he would become agitated, pace the floor, and his words would be harsh, vindictive, belligerent, and unreasonable.

"I have seen him on a number of occasions, when he would come, as it were, to a climax in his dictating on the life of Mrs. White, totally exhausted, tears flowing from his good eye as well as from the open socket while he wept bitterly. At such times I have seen him drop in his chair by his desk, and momentarily bury his face in his arms on the desk. Then as he swung his left arm in a gesture of utter despair, he would exclaim with three inflections, each more pathetic than the one before, 'I'm a lost man! I'm a lost man! I'm a lost man!' Frequently he would add, 'She was a good woman! I am gone! gone! gone!'—Pages 134, 135.

"It was almost more than I could take. As a result I decided to take his dictation with my back turned to him, without having to witness his anguish. In this way I was able to proceed with my work."

The poor man seemed to be controlled by some demonic power that made him fight Adventists while he loved them dearly. He seemed unable to say what he wanted to say and do what he wanted to do. He never found the popularity or the greatness that he was so sure he would find.

I hope it does not seem unkind to point out that Ellen White, as the Lord's messenger, had once written D. M. Canright, in a letter of warning, "You have wanted to be too much, and make a show and noise in the world, and as the result your sun will surely set in obscurity."

That is exactly what happened. Such is the tragic end of pride!

Yes, it must be a sad and terrifying experience to watch a star go out. On the other hand, it is wonderful beyond words to watch the Lord Jesus work miracles of transformation in thousands of lives. To see them drawing nearer the Saviour than ever before. Reflecting His image. Shining out in the night one by one. Taking the place of those who have slipped away.

Elijah added up a column of figures once and got only one. God added up the same column of figures and got seven thousand!

"Among earth's inhabitants, scattered in every land, there are those who have not bowed the knee to Baal.... God has in reserve a firmament of chosen ones that will yet shine forth amidst the darkness."—*Prophets and Kings,* pp. 188, 189.

"The careless and indifferent . . . were left behind in darkness, and their places were immediately filled by others taking hold of the truth and coming into the ranks."—*Early Writings,* p. 271.

But when a star of exceptional brilliance burns out, some may ask, "Does God have other lights like this? Does any other man possess the unique combination of talents needed for this particular place in God's plan?"

Possibly not.

Come with me back, past the beginning of time, into eternity. This planet, and those who would ride it, existed then only in the mind and plan of God. We see a great company of angels, and at their head, standing tall and straight, the mightiest, most beautiful being ever created. Son of the morning! He had no equal among the angels. God had created no other like him. He had been especially prepared for his high position, close to the throne, leader of heaven's choir.

The angels looked on in admiration. There, tall and straight and mighty, was their beloved leader. No other had ever been able to sing the praise of God so appealingly as he. No other could so eloquently tell the love of the Father. His words were like the brush of an artist upon the canvas. His voice was captivating in its modulations.

But then came the day when the angels were troubled. For now, it was said, This glorious angel had allowed strange feelings to enter his heart. God called it sin. Heaven had never before heard that word. Angels could not understand it. Sin. And in it, God said, were the seeds of death. The son of the morning, unless he turned from his strange course, must be banished from heaven.

Not he! The angels were confused. How could it be? Some other angel, perhaps. But not the son of the morning. Another angel might be replaced. But God had prepared no other like the mighty one who stood now in the distance, making his decision.

The angels watched and wondered and waited. Lucifer turned and saw them watching. And then, his decision made, he slipped down, down to do his strange and alien work. And the angels never understood—until Calvary, until they saw the son of the morning crucify his own Creator!

They watched beside the cross. They saw loving hands lay the Son of God in the tomb. They waited through the long weekend. And then, in the early hours before dawn, they saw a mighty being speeding from heaven. The whole earth shook at his approach. He had come to call Jesus from the tomb.

Who was this mighty one? It was their beloved Gabriel—the one who had taken the place of the son of the morning. Not created quite as beautiful as he. Lacking slightly in talent and eloquence of voice, it may be. But mighty in power. And his heart inviolate, perfectly reflecting the image of his Creator. Gabriel—standing daily beside the throne where Lucifer might now have stood.

And Lucifer, by his own choice, stood at that moment in

the shadows, furious because all his wicked devices had failed to hold the Saviour in the tomb!

Sin can never be explained. It is without explanation or excuse. It attacks all, the lowest and the highest, but especially the highest. Those with exceptional talent and preparation are its special targets. Men's hearts still are lifted up because of their beauty. Popularity is still a slippery road. And when a bright light dims, thousands may stumble in the sudden, unexpected dark!

Every man, high or low, must one day stand at the point of decision. Those who walk the heights of human acclaim must decide whether applause will be their master or their servant. Shall God or self be first?

God will still have His Josephs and His Daniels. God will find His Gabriel, should these fail. Somewhere, standing by, is someone that God can use. Not as talented, perhaps, Not as eloquent. But with a heart inviolate. The work will go on. Yet we might as well recognize that a few of the lights shining most brilliantly in this late evening sky, just before earth's midnight hour, will go out, never to be truly replaced.

And God Himself cannot prevent it, without making every man a slave. We need not be surprised. We need not stumble. For as long as men are free, there will be lights—brilliant, talented, gifted lights—that will go out in blackness and never shine again. Such is the mystery of sin!

But such is also the mystery of freedom. For only so long as men are free to sin are men free not to sin.

And so, with the eyes of the multitude upon them, those who walk in high places decide. No man can decide for them. Decision belongs to the soul alone. They may choose to follow the son of the morning in search of applause. Or they may push self aside and let Christ be King. We can only pray that Christ shall reign.

But if not—a Gabriel somewhere, is standing by!

Angel Tribute

I seem to see an angel pen
Begin to trace
The record of the work
That I have done;
And in the space
He writes the number of the souls
That I have won.

And then, with pen so eloquent, he tells
The sermons that the people said
God must have sent.
And as I watch, my glad heart swells
With joy to see the angel use
The very words that men have often lent
To tell their praise.

I look—how true the record—
For his pen describes the throngs
That came to hear those touching gospel songs,
But most to hear my words.

I seem to see again the wondering crowd
That only yesterday stood by in silent awe
As prayer—my prayer—was answered
And a stricken man was healed.
And yes—the angel writes

What I had scarcely dared opine:
They thought—the wondering crowd—
They thought the miracle was mine!

O angel, stay thy hand!
And write no more the record
Of my sins.
Write not my inmost thoughts of pride
For all the world to see!

The record that you trace
Upon the page, O angel scribe,
Is none of mine.
I did not win the souls
Or find the sheep
Or bring one lost one to decide—
It was His love!

The crowds came not to hear
My words, but His.
The miracles—O angel, write
No glory anywhere upon my page.
It all belongs to Him!

Write not the tributes that are falsely mine.
Write only this, that wondrous love
Reached down to me so deep.
Write that a joy untold is mine
To watch Him save the sheep.

His is the power, His are the souls,
And His the love that wins.
Write Him another tribute in eternity's glad theme,
But write no glory by my name—
It all belongs to Him!

A Bridge Too Far

Dr. W. E. Sangster was present at an anniversary celebration in Gloucester which had attracted many dignitaries. One clergyman on the rostrum made a particularly impressive appearance—not only because of the portliness of his figure and the red and black velvet of his robe, but also because of a striking gold cross that he wore suspended from a heavy watch chain. It was evident, all through the principal speaker's address, that the portly clergyman was bored by anyone's efforts but his own. But Dr. Sangster was horrified as he noticed, at one point, that the man had taken the gold cross off its chain and was cleaning his fingernails with it!

Frederick Speakman, who passes along the story, makes this comment: "We've all been in danger of that unconcern in the Christian Church of the latter days, laymen and cleric alike—with our loose thinking and our trifling with so much that the centuries have known was serious, with . . . the church just another competing organization, with worship become mostly sermon-tasting, with our amazing flabbiness in the disciplines of prayer and usefulness that alone can make God real to men! We've been sending faith on pretty errands trying to harness its eternal claims to cure our headache or give us more poise, stripping the gospel down to a mere Biblical barbiturate, a two-for-a-nickel sedative packaged for peace of mind! In all this we present inheritors of the Christian tradition stand perilously close to just that brand of irreverence—cleaning our fingernails with the cross."—*Love Is Something You Do,* p. 46.

I'm not so sure of the healing power of a cross on a chain, or even the reverence due it. But it's true that we do send the cross, the real cross, on many a trivial errand. We expect it to cure our headaches and our personality problems and our common colds. But we never even ask that it cure our pride.

Why is this? Is it because we still think of pride as a trivial, respectable weakness of humanity that is not serious enough to require any attention? What are we thinking of? Pride is what got us into this mess we're in! Pride is what shut Lucifer out of heaven! Pride is what will shut every one of us out too, if we don't get rid of it! We get all stirred up over murder and adultery and even malicious gossip. Why don't we get stirred up about pride? Do we think for a moment that God would cast pride out of heaven and let His Son die to free the universe from its curse—and then let it in again? Never!

"There is nothing so offensive to God or so dangerous to the human soul as pride and self-sufficiency. Of all sins it is the most hopeless, the most incurable."—*Christ's Object Lessons,* p. 154.

"God cannot connect with those who live to please themselves, to make themselves first. Those who do this will in the end be last of all. The sin that is most nearly hopeless and incurable is pride of opinion, self-conceit."—*Testimonies,* vol. 7, pp. 199, 200.

Pride is the essence of rebellion. It is both the root of sin and its contagious fruit. Pride is lethal!

Pride is the sin of Laodicea. And its pride is complicated by blindness. "Because thou sayest, I am rich, and increased with goods, and have need of nothing; and knowest not that thou art wretched, and miserable, and poor, and blind, and naked." Revelation 3:17.

Laodicea *doesn't know* she is poor, *doesn't know* she is wretched and miserable and unclothed. Laodicea *doesn't know* she is blind and *doesn't know* she is proud. That's why she is lukewarm about getting rid of her pride. That's why she is lukewarm about the lateness of the hour. That's why she is lukewarm about everything and everyone—even the Lord Jesus. Laodicea doesn't care because she *doesn't know*. And what remedy, what cure, can there be for "knowest not"?

Thank God there *is* a cure. But it involves the surrender of the proud heart. And that's rough medicine to take!

I don't know how you feel about the *National Enquirer*. Not only does it have the largest circulation of any paper in America, some people say it is also the most controversial. Others say you can't believe anything you read in it. A little checking has revealed, however, that at least some things it prints are true. So it may be that we ought not to conveniently write off every story it carries simply because of where it appears.

At any rate, the *Enquirer* of July 31, 1979, carried a most interesting article. Decide for yourself whether or not it has any merit. It quotes Morton Kelsey, a Notre Dame University professor of theology, as saying, "Most people in the modern world consider themselves too sophisticated and too intelligent to be concerned with demons and angels. They totally ignore the evidence around them. But in 30 years of study, I have seen the effects of angels and demons on humans.

"A demon in a human," he says, "is real—not a figment of the imagination. It is a negative, destructive spiritual force. It seeks to destroy the person and everyone that person comes in contact with."

So far I think we would all agree. But now notice what Professor Kelsey says: "There are several indicators of demonic possession: the person demands complete obedience from others; uses people rather than relates to them; seeks power rather than love; doesn't treat others as human; tries to dominate, and suffers from incredible depression and inner turmoil.

"The essential mark of the demon—and those possessed by demons—is total self-interest. He is dominated by this self-interest to the exclusion of everyone and everything else."

How about it? Is he right? Is the man who is *obsessed* by pride running the risk of being *possessed* by the author of pride? And if so, where is the line between *obsession* and *possession*? Can we expect to partake continually of the *spirit* of Lucifer without finally being *possessed* by Lucifer?

Remember D. M. Canright, who seemed to be controlled by a demonic power that wouldn't let him do what he wanted to do?

Did we really need Professor Kelsey to warn us of the danger? Hasn't the messenger of the Lord repeatedly cautioned us of just such a possibility?

"When we see men firm in principle, fearless in duty, zealous in the cause of God, yet humble and lowly, gentle and tender, patient toward all, ready to forgive, manifesting love for souls for whom Christ died, we do not need to inquire, Are they Christians? They give unmistakable evidence that they have been with Jesus and learned of Him. When men reveal the opposite traits, when they are proud, vain, frivolous, worldly-minded, avaricious, unkind, censorious, we need not be told with whom they are associating, who is their most intimate friend. They may not believe in witchcraft; but, notwithstanding this, they are *holding communion with an evil spirit*."—*Testimonies*, vol. 5, pp. 224, 225. (Emphasis supplied.)

"He who holds the truth in unrighteousness, who declares his belief in it, and yet wounds it every day by his inconsistent life, is surrendering himself to the service of Satan, and leading souls to ruin. This class *hold intercourse with fallen angels* and are aided by them in gaining the control of minds."—*Ibid.*, p. 142. (Emphasis supplied.)

"Sin is from beneath; and when it is indulged, *Satan is enshrined in the soul*, there to kindle the very fires of hell."—*Ibid.*, vol. 4, p. 345. (Emphasis supplied.)

I wish I could believe these statements are speaking of something that only rarely happens. But I fear they are not. "A great proportion of those who are supposed to be genuine will give heed to seducing spirits, and will turn traitors and betray sacred trusts."—Ellen G. White Comments, *S.D.A. Bible Commentary*, vol. 6, p. 1065.

"Give heed to seducing spirits." Does this refer to involvement with spiritism? Or are we giving heed to seducing spirits when we partake of the spirit of their leader?

Pride is not a little thing. It is not some trivial little weakness of humanity—if any weakness is trivial. When we toy with pride, we are toying with the basic characteristic of the great deceiver—that which caused his fall. Pride is behind the whole ugly show!

You and I, at this moment, are under the control of one power or the other. Either Jesus is in control—or Satan is. Either Jesus is enshrined in the soul—or Satan is. Either Jesus is stamping His image into our hearts—or Satan is stamping his. It is ours to choose.

The tragic thing is that it is possible to change leaders and not know it. That's what the inspired word says: "If you indulge stubbornness of heart, and through pride and self-righteousness do not confess your faults, you will be left subject to Satan's temptations. If when the Lord reveals your errors you do not repent or make confession, his providence will bring you over the ground again and again. You will be left to make mistakes of a similar character, you will continue to lack wisdom, and will call sin righteousness, and righteousness sin. The multitude of deceptions that will prevail in these last days will encircle you, and *you will change leaders, and not know that you have done so.*"—*Reveiw and Herald*, Dec. 16, 1890. (Emphasis supplied.)

Joseph Addison Alexander said it this way:

> There is a line by us not seen,
>   Which crosses every path;
> The hidden boundary between
>   God's patience and His wrath.
>
> To cross that limit is to die,
>   To die, as if by stealth;
> It may not pale the beaming eye,
>   Nor quench the glowing health.
>
> The conscience may be still at ease,
>   The spirit light and gay;
> That which is pleasing—still may please,
>   And care be thrust away.
>
> But on that forehead God hath set
>   Indelibly a mark

> By man unseen, for man as yet
>   Is blind and in the dark.
>
> Oh where is that mysterious bourn
>   By which each path is crossed,
> Beyond which God Himself hath sworn
>   That he who goes is lost?
>
> How long may men go on in sin?
>   How long will God forbear?
> Where does hope end, and where begin
>   The confines of despair?
>
> An answer from the sky is sent,
>   Ye who from God depart,
> While it is called today—repent!
>   And harden not your heart!

There *is* such a line. And millions will cross it. Some by deliberate choice. But many more will cross it by neglect, always intending to turn back. They do not *choose* disaster. They simply *submit* to it.

Every man is free to follow the son of the morning down the path of pride if he chooses. No bell will ring to tell him when he has crossed the line beyond which there is no return. No signal. No siren. No red light.

There is nothing to stop us from crossing bridge after bridge, leading us deeper and deeper into Satan's enchanted country. The soul is free. But each time we cross a bridge we take the risk that the bridge may not be there when we want to come back. We take the chance of going a bridge too far. Like Esau. Like Judas. Like D. M. Canright.

A bridge too far! And we may not know when we have crossed it. We shall only know that there is no way back. That is the risk—the terrible tragedy—of pride!

Pride! Of all sins the most nearly incurable. But You must cure it, Lord—and cure it in time! Or we're all lost!

Unmasked

Five-year-old Teri came to my door one morning deep in thought. She was trying to figure out an elusive mystery. "Which one is the real Santa Claus? Is it the one with the Chinese eyes? Or is it us?"

She was really perplexed. There was the Santa Claus in Macy's parade. There was one in each of the local department stores. There was one who had been touring the neighborhood. There was one that had impressed her as looking genuine. But he looked as if he might be from China instead of the north pole. Who was the real Santa Claus? Was it any of these? Or was it, as she was beginning to suspect, *us*—Mom and Dad and her sisters Cris and Mindy—all playing Santa Claus to each other?

What about the masks of hypocrisy? When the masks fall off, when the game is up, when there is no more pretending, who will be revealed as genuine followers of Jesus? And who will be exposed as counterfeit?

There was a time in ancient Egypt when it was not difficult to tell which was which. If you visited a home and asked your hostess for a drink of water and she apologized, explaining that all the water had somehow turned to blood—you knew. If you noticed that the home was infested with frogs—you knew. If for three days some homes were deep in darkness while others were brightly lighted—you knew that God had made a distinction between those who served Him and those who served Him not. And when finally you heard a great wail ascending from the land of Egypt, you knew that in many homes a death had occurred when the destroying angel had passed through. He had spared from the terrible grief only those homes where blood had been placed on the doorpost!

God had made a difference! And He will do it again!

Today it isn't easy to tell the true from the false. The tares are entwined with the wheat. God sends His rain on the just and the unjust. The wicked, as in David's day, still prosper. If this were not the case, Satan would accuse God of giving his people an unfair advantage. He would charge, as in the days of Job, that God's people do not serve Him out of love, but because of all the benefits He gives them.

But the day comes when once again a distinction will be made and hypocrisy forever unmasked. It will be a day of both happy and cruel surprises!

Imagine, if you will, what it might be like. A father is having a little talk with his son, reprimanding him for not living up to his father's high ideals. But suddenly he is interrupted. "Dad, what's wrong with your face? What happened to your face?" And the father turns away in embarrassment and shame. For he knows what is wrong with his face. He knows. And he knows that his boy knows. Those ugly spots that appeared so mysteriously are beginning to be painful. And they are really no mystery to him or his boy. For years the father has covered a prayerless life with a mask of piety. But now the mask is off. Revelation 16 is beginning to happen!

A talented woman, active in the church for years, tries to hide her inner panic as she lifts the phone and makes an appointment with her dermatologist. Something on her arms, she says. An emergency. She puts on a long-sleeved dress to hide the problem from anyone she might meet. But she knows all too well that it is not a problem for the dermatologist. The problem is that she has loved the world more than she has loved Jesus. And now Revelation 16 is happening—to her! And she never dreamed it would be so soon!

A mother looks up as her teenage son comes home unusually early. She says, "Look at your face! Been eating chocolate again?" But it isn't chocolate. It's Revelation 16. And they both know it!

A minister on Sunday morning is just ready to enter the pulpit. But he is arrested by a burning sensation on his forehead. No! Not there! He's had these ugly sores on his back all week, but they were out of sight. Like his hypocrisy. It's too late now. He'll have to go ahead with the sermon. But some in his congregation have read Revelation 16. And word spreads quickly. Before the day is over, the game is up. The whole congregation knows that their minister, who week by week has preached the cross to *them*, has failed to place the blood on the doorpost for himself!

And Revelation 16 could happen on *Sabbath* morning too! It will happen to everyone, high or low, inside the church or outside—it will happen to every soul that has not found in the Lord Jesus a sure hiding place!

There will be a great darkness over the land as Jesus leaves the most holy place, His work finished, every case decided. No longer will a Mediator stand between the guilty sinner and a holy God. Never again will He intercede for repentant men and women. Never again will He lift His wounded hands and say, "Father, My blood! My blood!"

Nothing now will hold back the judgments that a loving Father and Son have delayed so long. Thousands will curse God because of the terrible scourges. Judgments will not soften the hearts that Calvary could not reach. They shake their fists at the sky in anger.

Others rush to God's people and ask how they can escape the judgments of God. But there is no message for them now. The last plea has been made. The last tear has been shed for them. And the bitter wail rises like a mushroom cloud from a doomed planet, "It is too late! It is too late!"

Too bad, we say, for the mark-of-the-beast people. But that isn't the whole story. Thousands of others will be involved in that heart-wrenching cry. Those who didn't know Jesus. Those who didn't love Him enough. Those who intended to follow Him sometime but put it off too long. Those who knew that Revelation 16 would happen but didn't think it would be so soon. And those who were too proud to repent.

Those whose pride kept them from the saving, healing blood of Jesus!

Friend, how would you live today if you knew that before another Sabbath had passed, the mask would fall away and your family and friends would see you as you really are?

There will be some sad surprises when Jesus returns—when we see who is left behind. But thank God there will be some happy surprises too—as we see who is there to welcome Him!

The good news is that thousands are loving Jesus more each day—finding in Him the answer to their every prayer!

The good news is that now, at this moment, there is still time to know and love Him. It is not yet too late!

And the great news is that Jesus loves impostors and pretenders, even the phoniest of them. He wants to forgive them—and make them sons and daughters!

There is a delightful story about a young man of our time who, like the prodigal son, decided to leave home and see the world for himself. When his money ran out, he joined a friend, a man close to his own age, in the life of a beachcomber. Together the two roamed the tropical beaches, sometimes earning a little cash by diving for pearls.

But one day this son-turned-prodigal was mangled by a shark and died. His partner immediately sensed an opportunity for himself. He was of the same race as the son who had died, and much the same build. They had let their beards grow and resembled each other amazingly. He thought he could quite easily pass as the son. So he took his friend's clothes and personal effects, with what money he had, and started out for his friend's home. As he traveled, he tried to recall all that the friend had told him about his home and family.

At the door he was greeted by the aging father and welcomed warmly without question. It had been five years since he had seen his son.

But everything was not easy. First of all he must dress for dinner—something he had never done in his life. Fortunately a servant was there to lay out his clothes and help him with his bow tie. One does get a bit rusty about such things after five years. To make it still more difficult, the guests at dinner were a father and daughter. And the impostor son got the impression that he was expected to renew an engagement to the girl.

He had stepped into a completely new life. Table conversation. Family friends. Family prayers. Attending church. Concerts, lectures, and golf. But he managed to do quite nicely in the new situation, he thought—until one day at a restaurant he met a woman who had been one of his own companions in his beachcombing days. It was clear that he could buy her silence only with a payoff of generous proportions. What should he do in this difficult dilemma?

The young impostor had come to love his new home very much. And his affection for the father had grown beyond all he had ever dreamed. So he went to him and confessed it all. The old man said, "I guess I knew from the start that you were not my son, but I so longed for him that I was glad to have you in his place. And now, why don't you let me adopt you so that you can become my son legally?"

How like Jesus! He has known all along that we were impostors. He has seen through our phony pretending. But He has let us carry on our act. He has loved us anyway. And now all He wants is to forgive us and change us and make us His own—sons and daughters of the King!

Can we ever understand a love like that?

Total Eclipse

Why didn't Jesus go singing to His death—the way the martyrs did? Was He less of a man? Did He have less courage than they?

There was nothing unique, in His day, about being crucified by the Romans. On one occasion the Romans stopped crucifying Jews only because they ran out of wood for crosses. At the time of the destruction of Jerusalem, in A.D. 70, the crosses would be so thick it would be difficult to walk between them. That's the way the Romans were. There was nothing unique about a cross. To the Romans it was business as usual.

Jerome of Prague, we are told, "went singing on his way, his countenance lighted up with joy and peace. His gaze was fixed upon Christ, and to him death had lost its terrors. When the executioner, about to kindle the pile, stepped behind him, the martyr exclaimed, 'Come forward boldly; apply the fire before my face. Had I been afraid, I should not be here.' "

An enemy said of Jerome, and of John Huss, who was martyred shortly before him, "Both bore themselves with constant mind when their last hour approached. They prepared for the fire as if they were going to a marriage feast. They uttered no cry of pain. When the flames rose, they began to sing hymns; and scarce could the vehemency of the fire stop their singing."

Jesus was born to be crucified. That's why He came. Repeatedly He had told His disciples about His coming death—*and resurrection*. He had promised to meet them after His terrible ordeal. Then why did He shrink from it as He did? Did He forget that He was the Son of God? Did He forget the voice from heaven that more than once had testified to His identity? Did He forget what had so lately happened on the mountain of transfiguration? Hadn't the Father been with Him all these thirty-three years? Hadn't angels always attended Him?

But this time angels would not deliver Him. This time there would be no voice from heaven. And Jesus would not approach His ordeal with singing. Why? Because Jesus would die a different kind of death. He would die a death that no man on earth has ever experienced—yet. Jesus would die in the sinner's place. He would die the death that the sinner must eventually die—except for His sacrifice. And in that final death there is no hope of resurrection. No wonder Jesus didn't go singing to His death. This was the kind of hell that He walked into.

Picture it—if you can. A day more than a thousand years beyond this moment. The gleaming City of God, with all His people safe inside, resting on a vast plain where the Mount of Olives now stands. The rest of the planet feeling the tread of the enemies of God from all ages, living again, determined that rebellion still will conquer. Moving over the broken surface of the earth to take the city for themselves.

And then they are stopped in their tracks. Stopped by a moving panorama that their eyes cannot escape. A replay of their own lives. Every wrong decision. Every rejection of the call of Jesus. The foolish fragile bubbles for which they exchanged eternal life. It all appears as if written in fire!

And then, in panoramic vision, is portrayed what God has done, the incredible length to which He has gone to try to save them. Not an eye can turn away. Every watcher sees, in divine replay, the scenes of the Saviour's life. His birth, His boyhood, His ministry, His hands reached out in healing, His rejection by those He came to save.

Every eye sees the mysterious agony in Gethsemane, His betrayal to the mob, the fearful events of that night of horror. And at last, before the swaying multitude, the final scenes of His sacrifice are seen again. The Prince of heaven hanging upon the despised crossbeam. The jeering mob deriding Him. The supernatural darkness. The convulsing of the earth at the moment of His death!

Every person in that vast throng knows now why he is lost. He knows now that he is lost because he chose to be lost, because he rejected the life that the Saviour died to give him. He sees now that he has exchanged eternity for a moment of passion, a few years of wealth.

Every soul now bows before the Lord Jesus—not in repentance, but in acknowledgment that God is just in denying him life. Even Satan bows. "That at the name of Jesus every knee should bow, of things in heaven, and things in earth, and things under the earth; and that every tongue should confess that Jesus Christ is Lord, to the glory of God the Father." Philippians 2:10, 11.

But rebellion still would banish God from His throne if it could. Hearts have not changed. Satan makes one final attempt. He tries to stir up the armies of the lost to storm the city. But nowhere in that vast multitude, nowhere in the universe, is there a trace of sympathy for him now. He is exposed before all the worlds as the cruel instigator of senseless rebellion—and the polluted fountain of all tears. This is where his foolish pride has led him. This is where the determination to go it alone has led the multitudes of the lost!

And now the fire falls! Says the apostle John, "And they went up on the breadth of the earth, and compassed the camp of the saints about, and the beloved city: and fire came down from God out of heaven, and devoured them." Revelation 20:9.

It is all over. The price for sin has been paid—by those who were unwilling to let Jesus pay it for them!

Do you see now what hell really is? The flames, you say. True, those flames at the end will be very literal and very real and very hot. But those flames are to put the lost *out* of their misery, *out* of their hell. Hell is the mental anguish that goes before the flames!

Hell is separation from God. It is seeing what might have

been. It is knowing what heaven is like—and knowing it will never be yours. It is being at the bottom of the wall, outside the city—when you could have been at the top of the wall, inside. *It is knowing that you will never live again!* It is eternal death!

Hell is the price of sin. It is the price that Jesus must pay if He was to take our place. The flames are not the price. If they are, then Jesus never paid the price of sin, for Jesus never burned!

The price of sin was not the cross or the nails or the thorns on Jesus' head. It was not the humiliation or the taunting of those looking on. It was not the physical pain. So great was the pain of separation from His Father that the rest was hardly felt!

And the price of sin was not a three-day death and then a resurrection. If it were, we wouldn't need a Saviour. We could easily pay that price ourselves. The price of sin is to die with no hope of resurrection. And if Jesus on the cross was confident He would live again, then He didn't pay the price of sin. If on the cross He was comforted by the Father's presence, then He didn't pay the price of sin. For the sinner who dies the final death will have no comfort whatever—from anyone or anywhere!

Do you see now why Jesus recoiled with such horror, such nameless dread, from the ordeal before Him? Do you see why He was seized with such gloom? He knew so much of what was ahead. And His closest friends, though He had tried to tell them, knew so little!

As He led His men out across the brook Kidron that Thursday night and started up the mountain, how tenderly He cherished the last moments with those He loved! How they would need Him before this night had passed! And how He needed *them*—now! But they didn't know—and didn't seem to care!

They came to a fork in the path. If they took the path to the right, they could go on over the summit and to Bethany. But if they took the path to the left, it would lead to Gethsemane—and hell! How strong must have been the temptation to go on over the hill to the home of Lazarus and his sisters—and rest! But He took the path to the left—straight into hell!

No wonder He began to stumble! And it was not like Him to stumble. Remember that Jesus was a strong man, an outdoor man, a man accustomed to hiking all over the country. His companions couldn't understand. Something was wrong. He must be very tired. They must get Him to the garden, where He could rest!

Several times He stumbled—not because He was tired, but because the weight of the world's sin had rolled upon Him like a mountain. It was crushing Him. Think of it! Every one of my sins. Every one of your sins. And all the sins of everybody else who ever lived or would live on this planet! All at once! The punishment for every one of them falling on Him!

And listen! *Not one of those sins was His own!*

Tell me. Are you good at taking the blame for what other people do? Do you enjoy being identified with other people's mistakes—even insignificant blunders? Or are you quick to point out that they aren't yours?

I confess that if a page of messy typing were slipped into a manuscript of mine, it would be very, very difficult for me not to point out that I didn't do it. But Jesus? Never once did He remind His Father that my sins were not His. And a lot more than messy typing was involved. My sins alone were enough to crush Him. But *everybody's?*

The load that weighed upon Jesus that night included ugly things like murder and adultery and child abuse. Would you like to be thought guilty of abusing a chld? Would you be willing, even for love, to let people think you could do a thing like that? Yet never once did Jesus kneel and say, "Look, Father! I'm just *carrying* this sin, just *assuming* it. Don't forget that I didn't *do* this terrible thing!"

Maybe now we can better understand what Paul meant when he said, "For he hath made him to *be* sin for us, who knew no sin." 2 Corinthians 5:21.

And Peter said of Him, "Who his own self bare our sins in his own body on the tree." 1 Peter 2:24.

In His own body. In His own mind. The multiplied guilt of millions was already crushing out His life as He approached

Gethsemane. No wonder He stumbled! Not only was He carrying the weight of the world's guilt, but He was carrying it alone. The Father was withdrawing His presence. The Son must die the death of the sinner—alone, without comfort, without hope. That was the cup He must drink!

He enters the garden, and Satan is there waiting, ready to wrestle Him to the ground with his terrible temptations. "Look!" he whispers, "You're not going to come through this. Your Father hates sin, and You've identified Yourself with it. He'll never take You back. You'll never rise again. You're going to die forever!"

And Jesus digs His fingers into the ground, hanging on desperately as if to keep His Father from slipping away. What if what Satan said were true? What if the sin He had taken upon Himself should be so offensive to His Father that He could never take Him back? And the conflict in His mind was so fierce that Jesus would have died right there in Gethsemane if the angel hadn't come to strengthen Him!

Oh, friend, do you see? Do you see why the cup trembled in His hand? Jesus was not deciding to die for us till Sunday morning. He was deciding to die for us forever!

And do you see now why Jesus on the cross cried out to His Father, "My God, my God, why hast thou forsaken me?" His Father *had* forsaken Him. He had withdrawn every ray of His presence. Jesus must die alone. And He must die without seeing through the tomb. That was the cup! That's how much He loved you and me. Wonder of wonders! Who can ever understand it?

One question above every other needs to be answered by you and me. It is this: Who crucified Jesus?

The Roman soldiers, you say. The unbelieving Jews. Some say Pilate did it. Others say it was really Judas. Some place all the responsibility on Satan. And some put all the blame on Adam. Did we forget Caiaphas? And all the scribes and Pharisees and priests and rulers and doctors of the law who had been plotting His death?

Who did it? They all did!

But humanity is expert at shifting the blame. The Roman soldiers didn't know what they were doing. They were just carrying out a routine assignment. The people were misled and stirred up by their leaders. Pilate didn't want Jesus crucified. Neither did Judas. He was only trying to put Jesus in a position where He would have to free Himself miraculously—and then the people would make Him king and Judas would get the credit. Satan didn't want Jesus to die. He knew that the whole unfallen universe would hold him responsible if Jesus should die. He only wanted to make it so desperately unpleasant for Jesus that He would turn back from His plan to save men. Adam said his sin was the fault of Eve. Caiaphas argued "that it is expedient for us, that one man should die for the people, and that the whole nation perish not." And the religious leaders, almost to a man, had taken refuge in each other and said, "Have any of the rulers or of the Pharisees believed on him?"

Peter was preaching on the Day of Pentecost. Peter once so impulsive. Once so proud. Peter, who shamefully denied his Lord, said he didn't even know Him—and punctuated his denial with cursing. Peter once so timid, so afraid, hiding from the wrath of the enemies of Jesus. But now listen to him: "Therefore let all Israel be assured of this: God has made this Jesus, whom you crucified, both Lord and Christ." Acts 2:36, N.I.V.

"This Jesus, *whom you crucified!*" Does Peter realize what he is saying? Does he mean to make it quite that strong? Does he realize that his enemies are in his audience, listening to every word? Does he mean to stand up there with no visible bodyguard and accuse his audience of crucifying Jesus? More than that, does he mean to tell them that the Jesus they crucified *is the Son of God*? Yes, he means every word of it!

And what happened when he said this? Did his audience drag him out to a cliff and try to push him over? Did they stone him? No. "When the people heard this, they were cut to the heart and said to Peter and the other apostles, 'Brothers, what shall we do?' " Verse 37.

"This Jesus, whom you crucified." There was the secret of Peter's power that day. That was what the Holy Spirit drove home to the conscience. And it cut deep. That's what led to the conversion of 3000 in a day. That was the message of the

early church: *You crucified Jesus! And the Jesus whom you crucified was the Son of God! And God raised Him up!* That was the message that turned a pagan world upside down!

What made Peter so bold that day? What gave him such boldness that he could accuse his audience of crucifying the Son of God? The Holy Spirit, you say. And that is true. But there is more!

Peter, long before he stood up to preach that day, had wrestled and wept on his knees—most likely for many hours. He had been consumed, almost to death, by the terrible realization that it was *he himself* who had crucified Jesus! He was not pushing the blame onto the consciences of others without first having borne it himself!

Peter's denial of his Lord is not something to be excused. Peter wouldn't want it to be. But Jesus, always so full of compassion, understood Peter's confusion that dreadful night. Jesus knew that Peter meant it when he said that he would defend Him to the death. But the thought of Jesus' dying had no place at all in Peter's mind. Jesus was the Messiah. He was the Son of God. He would soon take the throne of David. Jesus could deliver Himself from any danger. Peter had seen Him do it more than once. He would not let the mob take Him. Peter was as confident of that as Judas. And see? See how the angry mob falls backward to the ground—as if dead? Jesus is in no danger. He is the Son of God. This may be the biggest night of all!

But suddenly Jesus *is* being bound. He *is* submitting to the mob. He *is* letting His enemies take Him away. He is doing nothing whatever to free Himself. And the horrible night speeds on, each moment of it shattering Peter's dreams and jolting wildly his confidence in Jesus. Could it be that He isn't the Son of God after all? Peter is desperately confused—and indescribably depressed. Why is all this happening? And in the midst of this turmoil he is asked about his relationship to Jesus. Why don't they leave him alone? But three times he is asked. He says he doesn't even know Him. And he curses. And the cock crows. And Peter remembers!

Just then Jesus looks at Peter. And in that look is no reproach—only compassion, only forgiveness. But in that look there is also a deep hurt. And Peter knows in that moment that what he has done has hurt Jesus more than all the curses of the mob, more than all the torture, more than anything the mob could do to Him!

Peter rushes from the hall. He cannot stand the thought of what he has done. He runs out of the city, up the hill, and finds himself in Gethsemane again, at the very place where Jesus prayed—alone—a few hours before. He can see the marks of the terrible mental conflict that his Lord endured while he, the boasting Peter, slept. He sees where Jesus dug His fingers into the ground. If ony he could die!

What Peter experienced that night is too intimate for us to know. But we do know that he came out of the garden a changed man. The proud Peter would never be proud again. His pride and self-sufficiency was gone. Now he was ready for the power. Now he was ready for a bigger drum!

And what did it? The knowledge that he, Peter, was crucifying his Lord!

It will do the same for us!

Us? We weren't even there. We aren't responsible. We didn't do it. Or did we?

Didn't Jesus die for our sins? Yes. That's why we claim forgiveness. He died in our place. Then it must have been our sins that crucified Him, our sins that crushed out His life. We cannot claim the benefits of His sacrifice without accepting responsibility for it! If it was not our sins that crucified Him, if our sins were not included, then our sins have no part in the forgiveness He made possible!

I know that pride rebels when it comes face-to-face with the cross. Pride stubbornly refuses to accept any personal responsibility for the death of Jesus. But pride can also be melted there. Pride can be totally eclipsed by the incredible love it sees there. And you and I will never know and love Jesus as it is our privilege to know and love Him until we realize that we, you and I—not Judas or Pilate or somebody else—are the ones who crucified our Lord!

Cyril J. Davey in his book titled *The Story of Sadhu Sundar Singh,* published by Moody Press, tells about Sundar Singh, a boy of India. He was almost fourteen when his mother died and his world collapsed. He was desolate, literally desperate. No one could comfort him. He knew he could not live without God. But it seemed to him that God had taken away the only person who could ever make Him real.

Sundar attended a Christian mission school—because the government school was too far away. But his father did not worry about the teachers making a Christian of him. He knew that Sundar was proud of his heritage as a Sikh. And besides, something about the Christian's Book seemed to make the boy strangely angry.

In spite of this, he had always been a quiet, courteous, and diligent student. But now, in his grief, everything changed. He became a violent young ruffian. And the kindness of his teachers only infuriated him. He hated them. He hated their school. He hated their Book. And he hated their Jesus!

And then one day he approached one of his teachers and politely asked him to sell him a copy of the New Testament. Little did the teacher suspect why he wanted it!

Soon Sundar was saying to his young friends, "Come with me. You are surprised that I should buy this Book. But come home and see what I do with it! How long I shall live I cannot tell you. Not long, certainly. But before I die I will show you what I think of Jesus and His Book!"

He led the way to the courtyard of his home. From the kitchen he brought a bundle of sticks and a tin of kerosene. He poured the oil on the wood and set it burning with a match. Then he took the New Testament from his pocket. Slowly and methodically he tore the pages from the Book one at a time and threw them on the fire. It was to be his last gesture of contempt for the Christian's Book!

Suddenly his father walked out of the house and thundered, "Are you mad, child? Are you beside yourself to burn the Christian's Book? It is a good Book—your mother has said so—and I will not have this evildoing in my house. Stop it. Do you hear? *Stop it!*"

Sundar bent down, stamped the rest of the New Testament into the flames with his foot, and entered the house without a word.

For three days and nights he stayed in his room. And then

the night came that was to decide it all. For three days he had known what he was going to do. Not far away he heard the sound of a train as it rushed toward Lahore and was gone. The next express would be at five o'clock in the morning. And if God had not spoken to him before then, he would go out and lay his head on the rails and wait for the train from Ludhiana to Lahore to end his miserable existence.

His mind must be clear this night. He went to the bathhouse and bathed in cold water for an hour before returning to his room. It was seven hours till the express would come through.

He prayed, "O God—if there be a God—reveal Thyself before I die!"

The hours passed.

At fifteen minutes to five he rushed out of his room. He entered his father's room and grabbed the sleeping man by the shoulder to waken him. He burst out, "I have seen Jesus!"

"You're dreaming, child," his father said. "Go back to bed."

But Sundar was not dreaming. He explained how he had planned to end his life. He rushed on with his story.

"A few minutes ago," he said, "Jesus came into my room. . . . And He spoke to me. . . . He said, 'How long will you persecute Me? I have come to save you. You were praying to know the right way. Why do you not take it? I am the Way.'"

Sundar went on. "He spoke in Hindustani, and He spoke to *me*. I fell at His feet. How long I knelt I cannot say. But when I rose the vision faded. It *was* a vision. It was no thought of mine that called Him there. . . . Had it been Krishna, or one of my own gods, I might have expected it. But not Jesus!"

He paused, and then spoke again. "I am a Christian. I can serve no one else but Jesus!"

His father said, "You are half asleep, boy!" Yet he knew too well that Sundar had never been farther from sleep than at that moment. He spoke sharply, "You *must* be mad. You come in the middle of the night and say you are a Christian. And yet it is not three days past that you burned the Christian's Book!"

Sundar stood rigid, looking at his hands. And then he said

with deep feeling, *"These hands did it. I can never cleanse them of that sin until the day I die!"*

No wonder he loved Jesus! No wonder he preached Jesus till the day he died! No wonder he made his way, almost every summer, into the forbidden land of Tibet, enduring the worst of persecution. But the more he was persecuted, the happier he was that he could suffer for his Lord. And then, from his last trip into Tibet, he never returned!

Your hands, and my hands, are unclean too! Not because we have burned the Book, but because they are stained with the blood of Jesus! We have crucified our Lord! Our fingerprints—yours and mine—are on the nails!

Can we ever be proud again—knowing what we have done?

"This Jesus, whom you crucified," said Peter. But he was careful not to drive his hearers to despair. He made it plain that in the heart of the One they had crucified there was compassion and forgiveness and hope—hope such as they had never known. For the same cross that reveals our *unworthiness* also reveals our *worth* in the sight of our Lord. We are *unworthy* but not *worthless*. Jesus paid an incredible price for each of us. Will we tell Him that He made a bad bargain? He must have seen in each of us possibilities that we have never dreamed—to be willing to pay what He did!

But to look long and earnestly at Calvary is sudden death to pride. It is both the certain cure and the only remedy. For we don't twirl any batons while we are on are knees—while we are gazing, transfixed, at the cross where the Son of God is dying!

How happy Jesus would be if He could look down and see the freeways of our hearts crowded with trucks—trucks loaded with stolen thrones and foolish pride, headed for Calvary! For the highest place we can ever reach is not the top of some pinnacle, high in the world's acclaim. It is low at the foot of the cross. It is only there, and only then, that we are ready for a bigger drum!

And Then the Drum

A French explorer, traveling in the Congo many years ago, noticed that everywhere his party camped there were piles of wood all around, neatly stacked, ready for a campfire. He asked the guide one morning, "Who does this? What are these piles of wood for?"

And the guide replied, "It's the chimpanzees. They are all around us in the trees. They are watching us right now. They saw us build the fire last night. They saw us build the fire this morning. And as soon as we are gone, they will come down from the trees and gather the sticks. They will put the little ones below, then the bigger ones, and then the large ones—just perfect, ready for a fire. All through these jungles you will find these piles of wood. They have everything right, except the fire. *They have no fire.*"

Wood but no fire! We have plenty of wood to kindle a fire that will sweep the world. We have the men, enough men to make the greatest fire the world ever saw. But the men need to be set on fire!

We have wheels too—all kinds of wheels. We have wheels to carry the fire to the corners of the earth. But there must be fire in the wheels! Said the prophet Ezekiel, "The spirit of the living creature was in the wheels." The Spirit of God must be in the wheels. Organization is not enough. Machinery is not enough. We need fire in the wheels!

What would happen if we had the fire? What would happen if we had the power? What would happen if we were all in love with Jesus? What if we would surrender to our Lord all that we are and all that we *can be*—and let Him set it afire?

We are missing so much!

"It is impossible to give any idea of the experience of the people of God who shall be alive upon the earth when celestial glory and a repetition of the persecution of the past are blended. They will walk in the light proceeding from the throne of God. By means of the angels there will be constant communication between heaven and earth."—*Testimonies,* vol. 9, p. 16.

Celestial glory! Walking in the light proceeding from the throne! Constant communication between heaven and earth! Do we have to wait for the persecution? Why couldn't this be our experience now?

Think of it! Angels our constant companions! Happy hearts and shining faces and loving voices sharing the everlasting gospel! The drums heard round the world, beating out the good news that Jesus is about to return! Thousands listening—and joining us to watch for Him!

Why not now?

When we are ready to put self aside—it will happen. When God can give us power and not be embarrassed by what we do with it—it will happen. When we are ready to use His gifts not to dazzle but to win—it will happen. When, like Elijah, we are willing to be nothing—it will happen. When, like John the Baptist, we are ready to beat our drums not for self but for the Lamb of God—it will happen. It is *then* that like the little drummer boy we can play our drums for Jesus and see His smile!

Elijah was confident, bold, and fearless—a man of power. But the secret of his power was his humility. What about the Elijah *people*? Will the secret of their power be anything less?

Have you ever wondered what would have become of the early church if the disciples had gone ahead on their own—without waiting for the power?

Could it be that our problem today is too much witnessing without the power? Too much introducing of Someone we do not know ourselves? Could it be that if we really knew and loved Jesus, we would have something to tell and something to say and something to live—and people would come to us and say, "Who is this Jesus who means so much to you?"

You remember the walk to Emmaus. What if you or I had caught up with those two grieving disciples and given them the same Bible study, using the same scriptures? Would their hearts have burned within them?

You say the power is in the Word. You say it's the Spirit who presses the truth home to the heart. That's true. And God speaks through channels that are not perfect. He used Pilate to preach a marvelous sermon in three words: "Behold the man!" Jesus indicated that even the rocks could preach if necessary.

But does that mean that the condition of the heart—the heart of the one who speaks—has nothing to do with how the message is received? Does that mean that God can work just as well through unconverted witnesses as through those who know and love Him? Does that mean that it makes no difference?

Listen to these inspired words: "When the theory of the truth is repeated without its sacred influence being felt upon the soul of the speaker, it has no force upon the hearers, but is rejected as error, the speaker making himself responsible for the loss of souls."—*Testimonies,* vol. 4, p. 441.

What do you think of that?

A family living at Shunem showed great hospitality to the prophet Elisha. They even built a little room and furnished it so that he might make it a quiet retreat whenever he passed that way. God rewarded the woman's kindness by giving her a son. But one day, when the son was old enough to be in the field with his father, he complained of being ill, and at noon he died.

The mother determined to go to Elisha for help. He was then at Mount Carmel, and the woman set out at once with her servant. Elisha saw her coming. He sent Gehazi his servant to meet her and inquire about her health and that of her family. Gehazi did as he was instructed, but not until the mother reached Elisha did she reveal the cause of her sorrow.

Gehazi was then instructed to take Elisha's staff, hurry to

the woman's home, and lay the staff upon the face of the child. But when he did that, nothing happened. No miracle. It was not until Elisha reached the dead child and prayed for him that the child was restored to life. Why? Why was no miracle worked through Gehzai?

A later incident in the experience of Elisha's servant gives us a clue. Naaman the leper had come to be healed. Elisha had sent him to wash in the Jordan seven times. Then Naaman, grateful to Elisha, wanted to give him an expensive gift. Elisha refused it. But Gehazi had no scruples about accepting gifts, and through outright deception obtained the gift for himself. You remember what happened. The leprosy of Naaman came upon Gehazi, and he was a leper till the day he died.

Does the condition of the heart make a difference? Evidently it does!

What is holding back the power that we so desperately need?

Jesus gave His disciples power to heal the sick and cast out devils. But a father brought his son, possessed by a demon, and they couldn't dislodge the demon. Why? Because of something they had been disputing among themselves by the way. And you know what it was!

Can you imagine a man swelled with pride and filled with the Spirit at the same time? It would be like filling Nebuchadnezzar with the Spirit while he was boasting, "Is not this great Babylon, that I have built?"

The power must be preceded by a surrender that is very difficult for a proud heart. "No man who makes any reserve can be the disciple of Christ, much less can he be His colaborer."—*The Desire of Ages,* p. 273.

"We cannot discern the character of God, or accept Christ by faith, unless we consent to the bringing into captivity of every thought to the obedience of Christ. To all who do this the Holy Spirit is given without measure."—*Ibid.,* p. 180.

Lloyd John Ogilvie says it so well: "Take him in! Accept him as the greatest *man* who ever lived! Revere him as the most penetrating psychologist who ever analyzed life. Mark the calendar B.C. and A.D. Plan your customs around his birth, death, and resurrection. Speak of the gentle Jesus, meek and mild. Paint portraits of him, write the libraries full of line and verse about him. Sing for him; preach about him. We will have done everything we can with human skill and duration—except one—made him the absolute Lord of our lives!"—*Drumbeat of Love,* p. 186.

Yes, that is pride's ultimate manipulation!

Do you know what the antidote for Satan's apostasy is? It is the exact opposite of its cause: "Christian humility is a wonderful grace—the very antidote to the apostasy of Satan, which has unholy ambition and every delusion that he can frame. The grace of humility through Christ Jesus will make an imperfect man discern his imperfections and make him meet for the inheritance of the saints, where God is all and in all."—*This Day With God,* p. 16.

Humility will heal the soul and open the floodgates for the power. But where do we find that grace that seems to elude humanity? We find it by standing close to Jesus, the Sun of Righteousness. Then, just as the light of a candle is not seen in the bright floodlights, we will not see our own light at all. But when we move out into the darkness to find the lost, it will shine brightly, guiding them safely to the greater Light!

Why is the power so lacking among us? One reason for our powerlessness is that we are so satisfied with our powerlessness. By our actions we say, "Thank You, Lord. Thank You anyway. But we're doing nicely on our own."

We have so little of the Spirit because we have learned to do without the Spirit. We have learned to depend upon our pushing and our pulling, our busy activity, our projects and our plans and our committees. And we run our committees on a word of prayer and a few hours of talk. Like trying to run a car on a few drops of gas. Someone has suggested that we ought to turn it around and make it a few hours of prayer and a word of committee!

The danger is that we shall be so satisfied with our toys and our computers and our robots that we shall just go on turning the crank and never know that Jesus is missing! The danger is that we shall go on boasting of our success and not know we have miserably failed!

Says J. R. Spangler, secretary of the General Conference Ministerial Association, "Success is when the Lord comes!" And he couldn't have said it better!

The trouble is that too many of us want success to come clearly labeled with our name on it. But it won't—not real success. When Jesus returns in the blazing skies, He will not stand on the cloud and make a speech saying that His coming is sponsored and made possible by so-and-so!

We don't need to be the way we are. The news of something God has done through somebody else doesn't need to spoil a man's day. It can bring him to his knees and break his heart and make his day more than it ever could have been otherwise. For every revelation of a man's littleness, if he will accept it, makes room in his heart for more of God's power. A power that he may never see—for his seeing would dilute it and spoil it. But a power that crowds all boasting out and lets the Lord Jesus work!

May God keep us from the terrible delusion that He works only through us. May He keep us from the littleness, the fatal jealousy, that questions everything God does through somebody else—and sees it as a threat. Such a man will turn with scorn from the miracles God works in other hearts. He will reject as spurious any vision given to another, any healing done through other hands. And such a man will miss the latter rain entirely because he is protected from it by his own handmade umbrella of jealousy. He wants the rain to fall on him and no one else—and by that attitude he is making sure that it will fall on others and not on him!

We have no conception, we haven't the slightest idea, of the great things God will do when one day soon He bypasses the machinery, turns off the robots, leaves the pride of men behind, and works His mighty works through broken, committed, surrendered hearts that are willing to say, "I am nothing. God be merciful to me a sinner!"

There is no other way to power, no other way to finish the work, no other way off this planet. Only as we are willing to be little can we make sure of a place in God's country, where only the humble will ever dwell and where only God will be first!

We have a message about Babylon. Babylon, we know, is the symbol of false worship. But it is also a symbol of pride, of go-it-alone religion. We may congratulate ourselves that our doctrines, our personal beliefs, are crystal pure. Yet what belief could be more corrupt, more alien, more antagonistic to the everlasting gospel than the idea that our own efforts can count one whit toward our salvation? That is the very basis of false religion.

It isn't cathedrals that have experienced so tragic a fall. It's people. God says, "Come out of her, my people." And it isn't because they are entrapped in architecture soon to be thrown down by the judgments of God. There has to be a more personal reason.

Could it be that "my people" includes us too? Could it be that we, God's own people, who carry the everlasting gospel to the world, have ourselves become so entranced with the great city we have built, with our accomplishments and our supposed successes, that we haven't noticed that we've been losing altitude? Is it possible that our own personal ship could crash on the same rocks from which we've warned others away?

"Come out of her, my people," the Saviour says. And we look up in stunned surprise. "Who? Me?"

God help us to gaze long and intently at the cross—the cross that pours contempt on all our pride—and say while there is still time,

Yes, these are the hands that did it, Lord.
I can never erase the shame.
It is only the red, red blood that You shed
That can make them clean again!

Of Harps and Drums

There must be something wonderful about a harp—something unique, something that we do not understand. Otherwise, out of all the many instruments of music that you and I have heard, and out of all those known only to the unfallen universe, why did Jesus choose the harp? Why did He choose the harp to present to every one of us, along with a crown, as we enter the city? He must have thought it best of all. And He must have thought we would agree.

That's why it hurts me to hear anyone say he doesn't want to play a harp. I think it must wound Jesus to learn that someone doesn't want the gift He chose.

Why didn't He choose the trumpet? Or the flute? Or the violin? Or the drum? I don't know.

Could it be that He chose the harp because, even when played alone, it can produce glorious harmony? The trumpet and the flute are excellent solo instruments. And they blend beautifully in a group. But they can play but one tone at a time. Used alone, they can produce no harmony. The same is true of the violin, except for double-stopping. There is not much harmony in a drum. And a mighty pipe organ, of course, would be a little awkward to carry around. So Jesus, for whatever His reasons, chose the harp. And I am glad.

Some of us may not understand His choice. We may think we would prefer the stentorian voice of the trumpet, the strong lead of the first violin, the power of the drum. Too many of us, here, want to solo, all by ourselves. We want always to lead. We want to be *it*. But no man in that city of gold will want to be first. Every eye will be on Jesus, and every heart forever captured by the wonder of His love. Those who are willing only to solo won't be there. And I wonder about those who don't want to play a harp.

David played the harp. And David was no weakling. He killed the mighty Goliath when no other in Israel dared to challenge him. And evidently the music of David's harp had a charm that we cannot sense through the printed page.

I think we know little about harps. We have heard them played skillfully, and sometimes not so skillfully. But are we to conclude that the harps of heaven are no better than the harps of earth—and those who play them no more skillful? I think we haven't yet heard the harp at anywhere near its best. And besides, have we ever heard an orchestra of harps—ten thousand of them?

"Upon the crystal sea before the throne, that sea of glass as it were mingled with fire,—so resplendent is it with the glory of God,—are gathered the company that have 'gotten the victory over the beast, and over his image, and over his mark, and over the number of his name.' With the Lamb upon Mount Zion, 'having the harps of God,' they stand, the hundred and forty and four thousand that were redeemed from among men; and there is heard, as the sound of many waters, and as the sound of a great thunder, 'the voice of harpers harping with their harps.' "—*The Great Controversy,* pp. 648, 649.

The sound of many waters. The sound of a great thunder. The voice of the harps! I can hardly wait. Can you?

In the meantime—we are the harps. God is either making music with our lives or He is not. If we let Him, even now, our lives can blend with other lives in a sublime harmony of worship. But if we resist the touch of His hand, if we don't want to blend, if we don't want to be a part of the vast symphony of worshiping hearts, if we want only to solo— then God and our fellowmen will find in us no answering harmony, no echo of the songs of angels, but only broken strings!

What will be the song in that day? First the song of Moses. The song of deliverance. The song of God's providence and

His care. And then the song of the Lamb. Louder, loftier, and more sublime. Echoing and reechoing through the corridors of heaven. The song of Calvary. The gospel in ten thousand harps. Jesus all in all!

How appropriate it is that Moses should be linked with the Lamb, for he was so much like Him! Moses, once the proud and arrogant commander of Egyptian armies. Yet he went out to herd sheep and got acquainted with Jesus. And he became the meek, humble, compassionate leader of Israel, one of the strongest men who ever lived. Once he had thought of an army as a collection of men to be directed by his power, played as a giant, living keyboard. But he learned to love his people much as Jesus loved them. He loved them so much that, like Jesus, he was willing to die for them forever. Yet tenderly he was made to understand that only Jesus could buy men back from the hell toward which they were marching.

And look who else is singing! Paul the proud Pharisee—Paul, who discovered he was really chief of sinners and followed his Lord, through storm and sea and the fury of demons, to Rome and Rome's death! Peter, so proud when he walked on the water. So repentant when he sank lower than he ever dreamed he could! Nebuchadnezzar—the proud king who finally decided, after a seven-year detour, to let God be first! Evidently there is hope for proud people—hope for those who surrender their pride!

But if those ten thousand harps were to strike the note today, would we be ready to join in the song of Moses and the Lamb?

Listen to these moving words: "Satan has an accurate knowledge of the sins that he has tempted God's people to commit, and he urges his accusations against them, declaring that by their sins they have forfeited divine protection, and claiming that he has the right to destroy them. He pronounces them just as deserving as himself of exclusion from the favor of God 'Are these,' he says, 'the people who are to take my place in heaven, and the place of the angels who united with me? They profess to obey the law of God; but have they kept its precepts? Have they not been lovers of self more than lovers of God? Have they not placed their own interests above His service? Have they not loved the things of the world? Look at the sins that have marked their lives. Behold their selfishness, their malice, their hatred of one another. Will God banish me and my angels from His presence, and yet reward those who have been guilty of the same sins? Thou canst not do this, O Lord, in justice. Justice demands that sentence be pronounced against them.' "—*Prophets and Kings,* pp. 588, 589.

But wait! There is hope! "But while the followers of Christ have sinned, they have not given themselves up to be controlled by the satanic agencies. They have repented of their sins and have sought the Lord in humility and contrition, and the divine Advocate pleads in their behalf. He who has been abused by their ingratitude, who knows their sin and also their penitence, declares: 'The Lord rebuke thee, O Satan. I gave My life for these souls. They are graven upon the palms of My hands. They may have imperfections of character; they may have failed in their endeavors; but they have repented, and I have forgiven and accepted them.' " —*Ibid.*, p. 589.

And there is still more hope: "The assaults of Satan are strong, his delusions are subtle; but the Lord's eye is upon His people. Their affliction is great, the flames of the furnace seem about to consume them; but Jesus will bring them forth as gold tried in the fire. Their earthliness will be removed, that through them the image of Christ may be perfectly revealed."—*Ibid.*

When God's universe is finally clean from the ravages of rebellion, will He admit once more the sin that caused the fall of heaven's top angel? Never! But, thank God, thousands are permitting every trace of foolish pride to be forever dislodged from their hearts, washed away by the blood of Him who has been hurt most!

In the song of Moses and the Lamb not one discordant voice will be singing, "Glory to me." Rather, with the mighty thunder of ten thousand harps, the song will echo and re-echo across the galactic valleys of limitless space, "Worthy, worthy is the Lamb!"